the stolen children
their stories

Also by Carmel Bird

Novels:
Red Shoes
The White Garden
The Bluebird Cafe
Cherry Ripe
Crisis

Short Fiction:
Automatic Teller
The Common Rat
The Woodpecker Toy Fact
Births, Deaths and Marriages

Writers' Manuals:
Dear Writer
Not Now Jack — I'm Writing a Novel

Anthologies:
Daughters and Fathers
Red Hot Notes
Relations

the stolen children
their stories

Including extracts from the Report of the National Inquiry into the
separation of Aboriginal and Torres Strait Islander children from their families

EDITED BY CARMEL BIRD

RANDOM HOUSE
AUSTRALIA

Published by
Random House Australia Pty Ltd
20 Alfred Street, Milsons Point, NSW 2061
http://www.randomhouse.com.au

Sydney New York Toronto
London Auckland Johannesburg
and agencies throughout the world

First published 1998
Copyright©Carmel Bird

National Library of Australia
Cataloguing-in-Publication Data

The stolen children; their stories: extracts from the Report of the National
Inquiry into the separation of Aboriginal and Torres Strait Islander Children
from their Families

ISBN 0 09 183689 1.

Aborigines, Australian – Children. 2. Aborigines,
Australian – Children – Biography. 3. Aborigines,
Australian – Removal. 4. Aborigines, Australian – Child
welfare. I. Bird, Carmel, 1940-. II. National Inquiry
into the Separation of Aboriginal and Torres Strait Islander
Children from their Families (Australia). Bringing them
home. III. Title: Bringing them home.

362.849915

Cover photo: Between Two Worlds: The Commonwealth Government and the
removal of Aboriginal Children of part descent in the Northern Territory,
Australian Archives.
Typeset by Asset Typesetting Pty Ltd
Printed by Griffin Press

10 9 8 7 6 5 4 3 2 1

This book is dedicated to the people of the stolen generations. The editor hopes it will be regarded as an apology for the sorrows inflicted by white Australians upon Indigenous Australians for more than two hundred years. The greater part of the royalties on this book will be paid to the people whose work appears in the section 'Stories'.

Carmel Bird's interest in the lives of Indigenous people goes back to her early years in Tasmania. Her novel *The Bluebird Cafe* tells the story of a Tasmanian child of mixed race who is accidentally murdered after being kidnapped. A radio play *In Her Father's House* is about the tragic life of Mathinna, an Indigenous Tasmanian girl who was briefly adopted by the governor of that state in 1841. Her recent novel *Red Shoes* follows the theme of child stealing, in this case white babies illegally adopted into a religious cult.

Acknowledgments

The editor thanks the storytellers for giving permission for their stories to be re-told in this book.

And thanks also Sir Ronald Wilson for his Preface, Henry Reynolds for his Afterword, Cassandra Pybus for editorial consultation, Camilla Bird and Brianna Harrison for editorial assistance, John O'Meara for editorial and technical advice, and Karen Menzies for her vital role in contacting the storytellers. Thanks also to Robert Manne, Martin Flanagan, Jack Waterford, Veronica Brady, Lang Dean and Marilyn Lake for permission to include their work and to Jan Mayman for permission to quote from 'Sorry Time'.

They are people to be treasured.
Kim Beazley

CONTENTS

Preface

The Report of the National Inquiry into the separation from their families and communities of Aboriginal and Torres Strait Islander children by compulsion, duress or undue influence is not an ordinary Report.

Most official inquiries are directed to the ascertainment of facts and the drawing of conclusions. Their reports record those facts and conclusions and stand as an objective record, to be absorbed by the mind.

In the case of the stolen children, the Report was different. Much of it is expressed in the words actually spoken to us by those who suffered personally from the processes of separation. They are words which were spoken from the heart to the heart. The Report must be read with an open heart and mind, and with a willingness to listen, and to listen intently.

To read the Report in this way has been difficult for some people. Some of them have attacked the Report as lacking in credibility, because in reporting on the effects of the laws, practices and policies that resulted in the forcible removals the Human Rights and Equal Opportunity Commission, did not require those who told their stories to 'prove' that they were true, as they would be required to do in a court of law. These critics must have expected the Commission to embark on a process of investigation so as to discover the evidence of wrongdoing that would stand up in court.

To these criticisms I offer the response that the report is not that kind of report. We were asked to consult widely throughout the nation and to listen to Indigenous peoples, Indigenous organisations, governments, churches and community organisations. Having consulted widely, we were to trace the relevant laws, practices and policies and then to describe the impact of those laws, practices and policies on the lives of people.

The terms of reference do not ask the Commission to identify offenders for prosecution or as possible respondents to civil litigation. The objective clearly is not retribution, but understanding and healing.

In any event, there is no reason to doubt the general authenticity of the stories we were told. Altogether, the Commission listened to 535 personal stories of forcible removal and had access to another thousand or so in written form. In general terms, each of those stories was corroborative of the substance of all the others.

Furthermore, the manner in which the stories were told underlined their general credibility. There was nothing routine about listening to them. Notwithstanding their general similarity, every one was special because it recorded the experience of a particular unique individual. I was filled with a sense of privilege and awe that I should be admitted to share in these dreadful secrets of the past. I could not doubt their authenticity as the storytellers reached into their memories and their pain, sometimes for the first time ever, sometimes for the first time in many years. At times, it was as if they were reliving the experiences of which they spoke.

In an effort to be faithful to the courage and dignity of those who came forward to tell their stories, we have, in writing the Report, retained as far as possible the actual words as we heard them, It seemed to us the least that we could do.

There is a further comment I should make about the telling and listening to these stories. The Commission became convinced that the process of storytelling was itself the beginning of a healing process. We have therefore recommended that those remaining stories we were unable to hear because of lack of time and resources should continue to be told to an appropriate authority. In this way, one aspect of the healing process could continue.

The Report argues that reparation can only begin when there is an understanding that comes through listening, followed by an acknowledgment of the shameful deeds of the past and a genuine expression of regret.

Reparation can then be followed through with practical measures designed to facilitate reunions, to ensure access to culturally appropriate counselling, to the provision of appropriate compensation and finally to a fresh approach to current laws, practices and policies dealing with the welfare of Indigenous children and juvenile offenders so as to ensure that unnecessary removals are not continuing to take place today.

The national Inquiry disclosed that many of our fellow Australians are still suffering from the wounds inflicted by past laws, practices and policies which, notwithstanding that they may have been devised with the best will in the word, were ill-conceived and led to gross violations of human rights.

It is not too late for the nation to gain release from the burden of this shameful part of its history.

Ronald Wilson
Perth
August 1997

Introduction

Marked by a cross drawn in ink at about the place where her navel would be, the child stands in the centre of the group of six tiny girls. Her companions look shyly, sadly, at the camera; but her eyes are downcast. She seems to be oblivious, or at least forgetful, of the photographer, concentrating on a ball that she cradles at shoulder level. This child, with her high-domed forehead and gently pouting upper lip, is an orphan among orphans—Australian children of mixed race.

The orphanage was in Darwin, and the photograph of the children appeared in a newspaper in the 1930s, because the Minister for the Interior was appealing for people in Melbourne and Sydney to take the children in, to 'rescue them from becoming outcasts'. This was part of a long-term government plan to assimilate Indigenous people into the dominant white community by removing the children from their families at as young an age as possible, preferably at birth, cutting them off from their own place, language, and customs, and thereby somehow bleaching aboriginality from Australian society. This attempt at assimilation was nothing but a policy of systematic genocide, an attempt to wipe out a race of people. How apt it is, then, that this beautiful child is carelessly and so distinctly marked with a cross at the centre of her being, as if to signify the ruthless severing of the umbilicus that connects her to her mother and her race. The person who made the cross has written underneath the picture: 'I like the little girl in centre of group, but if taken by anyone else, any of the others would do, as long as they are strong'.

It is a haunting picture, an image of the saddest and most tender vulnerability, already damaged, about to be further violated and sacrificed. This picture is an emblem of stolen children, and it rouses pity, outrage, grief and mourning.

> Sorry Time was eerie music, like a rising wind:
> the song of tribal Aborigines in mourning.
>
> Jan Mayman, 'Sorry Time'

National Sorry Day, 26 May 1998; this day of mourning for the tragedies and losses suffered by Indigenous people of Australia takes place on the anniversary of the publication of *Bringing Them Home*, a Report prepared by the Human Rights and Equal Opportunity Commission from material gathered during the National Inquiry into the Separation of Aboriginal and Torres Strait Islander Children from their Families. One of the recommendations of the Report is that Sorry Day should be an annual event to commemorate the history of the forcible removal of children from their families. The Report documents a terrible grief and loss, and highlights the troubled relationship that exists between Indigenous and non-Indigenous Australians. This relationship is a critical and dramatic element in our history, imbued with tragedy and sorrow, affecting the lives of all of us, and until it is fully examined, acknowledged and mourned, there can be no reconciliation. There was an Aboriginal Day of Mourning on 26 January 1938. Fifty years on, and the sounds of lamentation are louder and more insistent. The evils of the past always come back to haunt us, and to deny the past is to cast a dark shadow, to cripple the future, infecting it with the nature of those evils. In editing this book, I hope to contribute to the revelation of the meanings of our past, to make the stories of Indigenous Australians more accessible to everyone, and to inspire more among us to read and consider the entire text and the full implications of *Bringing Them Home*.

Many non-Indigenous Australians are conscious of the wrongs done to Indigenous Australians both in the past and in the present, and are active in their determination to discover ways to right those wrongs. In August

1996 the Governor-General, Sir William Deane, gave the inaugural Lingiari Lecture at the Council for Aboriginal Reconciliation in Canberra. He said:

> True reconciliation between the Australian nation and its Indigenous peoples is not achievable in the absence of acknowledgement by the nation of the wrongfulness of the past dispossession, oppression and degradation of the Aboriginal peoples. That is not to say that individual Australians who had no part in what was done in the past should feel or acknowledge personal guilt. It is simply to assert our identity as a nation and the basic fact that national shame, as well as national pride, can and should exist in relation to past acts and omissions, at least when done or made in the name of the community or with the authority of government.

Sir William made it clear that the present low self-esteem and poor quality of life of many of our Indigenous people flow from the events of the past. 'The dispossession, the destruction of hunting fields and the devastation of lives were all related. The new diseases, the alcohol and the new pressures of living were all introduced.' The devastation of lives is the subject at the centre of the Report *Bringing Them Home*. It is a sad footnote to the Governor-General's 1996 speech that in 1997 he was moved to say, as the gap between Indigenous and non-Indigenous people appeared to widen: 'I weep for our country'.

Bringing Them Home is part of the examination of our past, its terms of reference being set down by the then Attorney-General, Michael Lavarch, in August 1995 when he asked the Human Rights and Equal Opportunity Commission to consult widely among the Australian people, in particular among Aboriginal and Torres Strait Islanders. The Attorney-General asked the Commission to trace past laws, practices and policies that resulted in the separation of Indigenous children from their families by 'compulsion, duress or undue influence'. He asked that it examine the present laws and practices available to Indigenous people affected by separation, including those laws relating to access to family records. He asked that the Commission examine the principles relevant to determining the justification for compensation for people affected by separation; to examine current laws relating to the care of Indigenous people; and to advise on necessary changes to these laws. He said that the 'principle of self-determination' by Indigenous people must be taken into account. It is a sad and telling fact that the Attorney-General should have had to draw attention to the need for self-determination of Indigenous people. But he was right, for the paternalism of the old Empire has not entirely disappeared in Australia in the 1990s. The need for self-determination is stressed at the end of the Report. In the words of Mick Dodson, Aboriginal and Torres Strait Islander Social Justice Commissioner, speaking on self-determination in juvenile justice programs: 'The standing of Aboriginal and Torres Strait Islander parents, families and communities to actively participate in and shape juvenile justice programs, which have such a disproportionate impact on our children, should be beyond question'.

So many things should be beyond question; so many things are not.

The questions now raised by the Report will never go away. They will haunt Australia until they have been understood and answered. Like the wind of Jan Mayman's 'Sorry Time' quoted earlier, these questions will rise and rise until Australia answers them and discovers ways to make good in the present the errors committed in the past. There is no escape from this fact. The past is not past. The past, the present and the future are, as they always are, part of each other, bound together. We cannot change the past, which cannot be undone; we may be able, by generosity of imagination and spirit, to change the future for the better, to act in a more enlightened and more humane manner, with greater dignity and true compassion. I write this Introduction not as a social historian, not as an anthropologist, not as a psychologist; I write only from an ordinary person's observation and understanding, from my heart, without sentimentality, and from my own moral imagination of the events and their significance. I felt compelled to collect the stories of the stolen children, separate them from the other material in the Report, and present them in this way with simplicity, clarity and compassion. They are documents of a unique kind, and I have chosen to place them among other documents which relate to them, reflecting on them, commenting on them in direct and illuminating ways.

When I read the stories of the stolen children I was very moved and I was awed by the dignified responses to hardship. I was, at the same time, reminded of the many stories everywhere of people in adversity, their courage and grace. And I found a redemptive quality in the stories themselves, in the act of telling both for the storytellers and for the listeners.

Many Australians are aware of the general meaning of the Report, having been alerted to it by newspapers, and particularly by television. We saw and heard the impassioned speeches of Sir Ronald Wilson, President of the Commission, and of Mick Dodson, Aboriginal and Torres Strait Islander Social Justice Commissioner. We saw the Leader of the Opposition, Kim Beazley, weep in Parliament the day after he first read the Report. We saw, to our shame, the Prime Minister, John Howard, refuse to apologise on our behalf to Indigenous people for their tragedy and sorrow, and we saw and registered, in fact felt, the shock that this refusal caused to Indigenous people. The refusal was a depth charge, and in the face of it Indigenous people responded with a dignity that could only inspire awe and an unbearable grief. As a result of the public discussion of the Report, many people bought copies and read them.

In December 1997, the Federal Government made its formal response to the Report. No apology has been offered by the government on behalf of the Australian people, but $63 million, to be spent over four years, has been set aside to promote the health and welfare of Indigenous people, and to support the repair of language and culture within Indigenous communities. There is an emphasis on effecting the reunion of families. But the deep and urgent wish of Indigenous people for an apology has not been fulfilled. Some of the state premiers have apologised, and some, although not all, churches—which were the agencies controlling many of the orphanages—have also apologised, expressing a profound regret and great sorrow, but the statement of apology from the Federal Government remains unsaid.

The Report is a document of some seven hundred pages, and costs more than many Australians can afford to pay for a book. Six months after its release, copies of *Bringing Them Home* were still unavailable in suburban libraries, and it was therefore inaccessible to the public for consultation or loan.

People were moved and to a certain extent informed by what they saw on television and in newspapers at the time of the publication of the Report. And news reports continue to keep us informed of the government and public response to the Report as time goes on. In fact some of the material I have collected here is only part of the narrative, because the story develops as time moves on. But the news media are ephemeral, and it was clear to me that unless people could have more ready access to the material in the Report, they would remain largely uninformed of its details, the true fabric of the matters in question. The Report not only contains stories of the denial of basic human rights; it alleges attempted genocide of Indigenous people of this country. We all need to know how such an allegation could be made. We need to know, for instance, the fact that in 1841 the Protector of Aborigines in South Australia actually presided over a massacre of thirty Indigenous people.

The findings of 1948 International Convention on the Prevention and Punishment of the Crime of Genocide came into force in Australia in 1951. One of the definitions of genocide is: 'the forcible transferring of children of a group to another group'. A state cannot excuse itself by claiming that the practice of genocide was previously lawful under its own laws or that its people did not (or do not) share the outrage of the international community.

White Australians need to read the stories of the people who suffered systematically and in so many ways at the hands of white Australians, principally of earlier generations. Indigenous people told their stories to the Inquiry and many of these stories are quoted in the Report. The courage, dignity and generosity, as well as the tragedy, of these storytellers shines out in their words, delivered from the heart and written in tears.

When I read the Report it became a matter of passionate urgency to me that the oral histories told in it should be made accessible to everyone.

People in other countries wished to know the stories I had read in *Bringing Them Home*. Of all the means of making the stories known—including publishing them on the Internet at <http://www.austlii.edu.au/au/special/rsjlibrary/hreoc/stolen/>—collecting them in a small book seemed to me to be the simplest and, in the long run, perhaps the most effective. I realise that images are in many ways more immediately powerful than printed words, that television and film are the key media in promoting a message to the world. But I think that a small and portable paperback book is still a useful storytelling tool, a carrier of messages. Reading a book is a private experience, a perfect way to receive the intimate and personal oral histories of these courageous and sorrowful people. If all the machines shut down, if the systems fail, so long as the sun shines, or we can light a candle, a few people may be able to shelter in some corner of the globe and read the stories in books. Books may be rapidly becoming drab, outmoded technology, but they have the potential, in their simplicity, to be the great survivors, in the end. A bit like the cockroaches, supposedly the lifeform that will survive a nuclear holocaust, a few books may still be bearing their messages when everything else has melted. It doesn't take much to get a book to work.

Most of the people whose stories are collected here first saw their stories in print in *Bringing Them Home*. They are people who were brutally and wrongfully separated from their mothers, their fathers, their families and communities when they were very young, people whose attachment to their own contexts were severed and destroyed. Remembering their lives, telling their stories to the Inquiry was difficult and heart-rending for them. Seeing the stories in print was a new and shocking confrontation with the horrors of the past. Several of these people have agreed to republish their stories in *The Stolen Children: Their Stories*, hoping that the stories will reach a wider audience, and help to convince all Australians that an apology is due to those who have come to be known as the stolen generations. Something I understand but deeply regret is that a few of the people whose stories are published in the Report were unable to face the experience of seeing the story reprinted here, and so their stories have had to be omitted. One of the storytellers, Carol, requested that the version of her story published here should be more detailed than the version included in the Report.

Most of the storytellers were interested in the idea of this book as a means of bringing their experiences to the consciousness of all, and were eager to cooperate. I wrote to the storytellers and asked them for permission to reprint their stories. Some of them, when they rang me, told me they had been to the library to check me out. They knew where and when I was born, and the names of some of my family, and the titles of my books. The experience of receiving their permission was unlike any previous experience I have had when putting together an anthology of other people's writing. These writers had already consulted their brothers and sisters before phoning me, and the phone calls we had were long and warm and very friendly and funny and sad. In some cases I did not speak to the storyteller, but to a member of their extended family. Some of the stories here were not included in the original Report, but are further documentation of the sadness of much of our history.

When people tell their stories, they usually enjoy feeling proud, and delight in being named and in claiming their own history. Not so the stolen children. The names under which these stories appear are not the real names of the writers. This is because the writers feel they must remain anonymous so that they cannot be identified as the people who have suffered as they have suffered. Their friends, employers, families might see them differently if they knew who they really were. This anonymity is yet another tragic element in this deep, vast tale of pain and sorrow that is a central part of the story of our country.

I would have liked to include photographs of the people who told the stories, pictures to illuminate and illustrate the stories, but of course that was not possible. The people must remain not only nameless, but faceless. Neither was it possible to give biographical details of the writers, as is usually the case in an anthology of stories. The real people behind the stories of the stolen children must continue to remain anonymous, to exist in the shadows of our history, until such time as Indigenous and non-Indigenous people in Australia are one, until our differences are reconciled, until the past is examined and mourned, and we can move on.

It is a commonplace notion that severe loss in any form has to be confronted, examined, acknowledged, discussed, exposed before a process of emotional and even physical healing can begin. One of the most powerful and effective ways people have of recovering from loss is the telling of the personal stories associated with the loss. The Church offers the confessional as part of this process; in modern society many people seek the help of counsellors and psychiatrists to whom they can unburden their souls, to whom they can tell their own stories of loss and pain. Listen to me, we say, let me tell you what has happened to me, let me tell you my story. If I can make you understand me, I may better understand myself. When people told their stories to the Inquiry many of them found that the act of telling was personally therapeutic. The act of listening is the other part of telling; you can't really tell a story unless somebody is listening. And in this case the listeners have as much at stake as the tellers. If Australia will listen to the stolen children and take their stories in and let those stories live in the consciousness of the country, this country will begin to heal the wounds of over two hundred years of deliberate and unconscious abuses of human rights.

I am indebted to Karen Menzies, a social worker who has acted as an intermediary between myself and the storytellers, for her sensitive under-standing, patience and insight. Without her help it would not have been possible for me to compile this anthology. And I am also profoundly grateful to Sir Ronald Wilson for writing a Preface for the book, and to the historian Henry Reynolds for writing an Afterword that sets out in brief the history of white supremacy and racial discrimination that characterised the 'settling' of Australia by Europeans, and that is still ingrained in our society. Martin Flanagan wrote 'Brother' particularly for this book, and Veronica Brady's piece was also specially written for the 'Perspectives' section. Robert Manne, Marilyn Lake, Lang Dean and Jack Waterford donated their published writing. I have placed these alongside extracts of speeches made in Parliament at the time of the tabling of the Report. The section 'Perspectives' could have been a vast, almost unending collection of responses to the Report, but I have selected just a few pieces which seem to me to form a kind of frame for the stories of the stolen children themselves.

No two words strike deeper into the human heart than the words 'stolen children'. Nothing is more valuable to us than our children, nothing so irreplaceable, so precious, so beloved. The history of white Australians is marred by children lost in the bush, children spirited away by unknown agents. The stories of these children have become the stuff of myth, icons of horror, and they ring with the notes of darkest nightmare. How must it be, then, to be such children, stolen children. How must it be to be children who have been snatched from their mothers and systematically stripped of culture, language, rights and dignity? To be such children who grow to be an adults within the very society that visited these crimes upon them. Yet the storytellers in this book are distinguished by a courage and a generosity that speaks with the voice of grace.

The conjunction of the words 'stolen' and 'children' is a horror for both the child and the mother. Etched into the stories collected here are the grief and suffering of the mothers. As Murray says in his journal: 'the worst thing that could ever happen to any woman black or white was to have her children taken from her'. Many members of the stolen generations suffered first as children who were taken and later as mothers whose children were removed.

The stolen children in this book speak of a feeling of emptiness, of having a sense of a hole in their hearts as they recall their loss of family, language, culture, identity. They catalogue the abuses they suffered at the hands of white families and missionaries, but the original wound is that which was inflicted at the moment they were torn from their mothers. Sometimes this happened with the mother's consent, the family being tricked into believing the separation was for the good of the child who would go away and be nurtured and educated and even loved. The tragic irony of this is brought out in 'Anne's Story'.

Sometimes it is the small details that have been etched in a child's memory that emphasise the horror of what happened to these children. One such detail is not in this book because the writer was one of those who could not bear to repeat the experience of seeing her story in print for a second time. However it is a detail that returns to me constantly for its simple and awful symbolism. This girl was sent to a white family at Christmas time. The daughter of the house received the gift of a bride doll, while the Indigenous child received a Raggedy Ann. A similarly striking incident occurs in 'John's Story'. When they arrived at the orphanage the small boys each carried a little suitcase containing only a Bible which was their treasure and which somehow gave them a kind of identity. The first thing they had to do, before having their heads shaved, was to cast their little suitcases, Bible and all, into a bonfire.

When you read the stories of the stolen children you will begin to know and feel how life has been—how life is—for many of the Indigenous people of Australia, people who were taken from their families as tiny babies or as children, and you cannot fail to be moved. And don't imagine that the children of today are immune. Part Six of *Bringing Them Home* is titled 'Contemporary Separations' and begins with a quotation from the Aboriginal Legal Service of Western Australia: 'The fact remains that Aboriginal children are still being removed from their families at an unacceptable rate, whether by the child welfare or the juvenile justice systems, or both'.

The wealth of evidence given to the Inquiry showed that the methods and practices in the removal and separation of Indigenous children from their families across Australia were similar in all regions of the country. The children could be taken away at any age, and many of them were taken from their mothers at birth or in very early infancy. Most of the children so taken were put into institutions where the other children were mostly Indigenous, of mixed race, and where the staff were non-Indigenous. If a child was adopted or fostered out to a family, that family was usually white. The objective of all this activity was to absorb the Indigenous children into white society, to force them to forget and deny their Aboriginal heritage and blood, and to bring about, within a few generations, a form of breeding-out of all Indigenous characteristics.

The children thus suffered contempt and denigration of their heritage, their own nature, and often the presence of Aboriginal blood was denied. They would be told that their parents were dead or had rejected them, and family members were unable to contact the children, or even to know where they had gone. Letters to and from the children and their true families were suppressed by the authorities; parcels of clothing and toys sent were never received. Children were severed from their roots, denied access to the true nourishment of their spirit, and were at the mercy of institutions or strangers. Children were exploited in every way, and were subjected to psychological, physical and sexual abuse. It is clear that subsequent generations continue to suffer the effects of the separations of the earlier generations, and that these separations are largely to blame for the troubled lives of many Indigenous Australians today. The complex, ongoing and compounding effects of the separations result in a cycle of damage from which it is profoundly difficult to escape. There is a theme of helpless sorrow running through these stories. There is a mounting theory that all Australians must learn to hear and to acknowledge.

Throughout the Report there are many short quotations from members of the stolen generations, as well as longer stories. Within both kinds of narrative there are moments when the reader must pause, draw breath, re-read a sentence in horror and in the hope of disbelief. Embedded in the Report's short explanations of the quotations from the words of the stolen children, are arresting little sentences that will chill you to the bone. Taking one of these at random: 'woman taken from her parents with her three sisters when the family, who worked and resided on a pastoral station, came into town to collect stores'. In that description of a life lies the sharpest tragedy and horror. The children are no more than a commodity; the authorities can simply take them from their parents who are going about their ordinary business in the town. I put myself imaginatively in the position of any of the people in this drama—the parents, the children, the police—and every position is intolerable. The situation itself is intolerable. I think that perhaps imagination is one of the most important and powerful factors in the necessary process of reconciliation. If white Australians can begin to imagine what life has been like for many Indigenous Australians over the past two hundred years, they will have begun to understand and will be compelled to act. If we read these stories how can we not be shocked and moved by stories such as the following?

In Confidential evidence number 528, given to the Commission, a man who was removed from his family in the 1970s, when he was eight, and who suffered sexual abuse in the orphanage and in foster homes organised by the church, said that he is still so frightened of the welfare system that he is afraid to have children of his own, and is unable to show love to others.

> There's still a lot of unresolved issues within me. One of the biggest ones is I cannot really love anyone no more. I'm sick of being hurt. Every time I used to get close to anyone they were just taken away from me. The other fact is, if I did meet someone, I don't want to have children, cos I'm frightened that the welfare system would come back and take my children.

It is surely a terrible irony that a system described as 'welfare' is cast in this man's mind (and in the minds of many other Indigenous people who told their stories to the Inquiry) as a monster that will invade his life and steal his children. Many of the short entries from confidential submissions contain phrases of a poignant wistfulness that is so very sad: 'I've often thought, as old as I am, that it would have been lovely to have known a father and a mother, to know parents even for a little while, just to have had the opportunity of having a mother tuck you into bed and give you a good-night kiss—but it was never to be'. The writer of that sentence in Confidential submission number 65, was fostered at two months of age, in 1936 in Tasmania. And a woman who was sent to the Cootamundra Girls' Home in the 1950s gives us in Confidential submission number 332 a vivid picture from her memory: 'I remember all we children being herded up, like a mob of cattle, and feeling the humiliation of being graded by the colour of our skins for the government records'.

There can be no disbelief; these are true stories, the stories of the descendants of the original inhabitants of this country. They reveal a society that tolerated the harshest cruelties, and that denied the existence of these cruelties, a society that hoped the problem of our Indigenous people would disappear, hoped that the people themselves would disappear, dissolve into the background like images in a fading photograph.

If you repeat a lie often enough it comes to be believed, but then if you keep repeating it on and on, it begins to be exposed for the lie that it is. I am a white Australian of Celtic background. I grew up in Tasmania with the story that the whole race of the Tasmanian Aborigines had been killed off last century. During my early life, the lie had been told too often, and the truth was beginning to get out, but slowly and very painfully. Genocide was attempted in Tasmania in the nineteenth century, but it failed. (Forcible removal of Indigenous children from their families occurred during two periods in Tasmania. The first began with the European occupation of Tasmania in 1803 and lasted until the middle of the nineteenth century. The second started in the 1930s with the forcible removal of Indigenous children from Cape Barren Island under general child welfare legislation and continues into the present. However, in more recent times welfare practice in Tasmania has regarded removal as an absolute last resort.)

The Indigenous people of Tasmania are very much alive today. The history I was taught, however, claimed that all Indigenous Tasmanians had been successfully eradicated by 1876 when Truganini died. Fearing her dead body would be seen as a curiosity and a commodity to be dissected and examined by scientists, Truganini said as she was dying: 'Don't let them cut me up, but bury me behind the mountains'. Her state funeral was farcical as the coffin was empty. Her body had been already buried in the chapel in the Hobart jail. Two years later it was exhumed and boiled and reduced to a skeleton that was stored in a wooden crate in the museum. Years later, during a clean-up at the museum, the crate was about to be thrown out. Suddenly someone realised it contained the bones of 'the last Tasmanian'. These bones were then assembled and put on display in the Tasmanian Museum and Art Gallery.

When I was a child I saw that skeleton. It seemed to me to be incredibly tiny, a waif of a skeleton in a glass case. It was taken off display in 1947. In 1976 the bones of Truganini were cremated and the ashes scattered in the

Southern Ocean. The story of the Indigenous Tasmanians is part of the story of the attempted genocide of the Indigenous people of Australia, and the stories of the stolen children are another part of that story.

I went to school in Tasmania with some girls who lived in an orphanage. The fact that they were known as orphans set them apart as different, yet it was not until I met some of them decades later that I realised they were Aboriginal. I imagine that this, my experience, is not unusual for white Australians of my generation. When I read *Bringing Them Home* I realised that the baby boy mysteriously adopted by friends of my parents was a child of mixed race. I was envious of his tight curly hair. I recall that he was very loved and nurtured by his adoptive family, and it is clear from some sections of the Report that not all Indigenous children who were removed from their own families suffered at the hands of their adoptive families. There remains, however, the tragedy of the loss of language and culture to any children cut off from their own people.

The Indigenous people of Tasmania had not, after all, disappeared. The Indigenous people of Australia and the islands of the Torres Strait will never disappear. They belong here, they have an indisputable right to be here in the full dignity of their humanity, and to contribute in confidence and joy to the future of this country. Listen to their voices.

Carmel Bird
Melbourne
Australia Day, 26 January 1998

The Stories

THE FOLLOWING STORIES ARE written just as they were told to the Inquiry. The names of the authors are the false names used in *Bringing Them Home* for the purpose of preserving anonymity and protecting the privacy of the authors and their families. Paul, Murray and Carol have added to their stories, and the stories of Anne and Donna are two which were not included in the Report. Donna writes under her true name.

All names appearing in the following section have been changed to protect the innocent.

I
Paul's Story

IN THIS ACCOUNT OF his life Paul has expanded on the version that was published in the Report *Bringing Them Home*.

This is a story where the colour of the boy's skin and the shape of his face are constantly examined by others in the hope that, by some trick of the light, the boy will emerge as non-Indigenous. When he is reunited with his mother as an adult, he realises that he bears not only his own pain, but also that of his mother. The story is Confidential submission number 133, and it is the story of a life in which numbers played a big part. The opening sentence draws dramatic attention to this fact, and is one of the sentences over which readers might pause and reflect. One of the most effective ways to remove a person's identity and dignity is to refer to them only by a number.

FOR EIGHTEEN YEARS THE State of Victoria referred to me as State Ward No 54321.

I was born in May 1964. My Mother and I lived together within an inner suburb of Melbourne. At the age of five and a half months, both my Mother and I became ill. My Mother took me to the Royal Children's Hospital, where I was admitted.

Upon my recovery, the Social Welfare Department of the Royal Children's Hospital persuaded my Mother to board me into

St Gabriel's Babies' Home in Balwyn…just until Mum regained her health. If only Mum could've known the secret, deceitful agenda of the State welfare system that was about to be put into motion—eighteen years of forced separation between a loving mother and her son.

Early in 1965, I was made a ward of the State. The reason given by the State was that, 'Mother is unable to provide adequate care for her son'.

In February 1967, the County Court of Victoria dispensed with my Mother's consent to adoption. This decision, made under section 67(d) of the *Child Welfare Act 1958*, was purportedly based on an 'inability to locate mother'. Only paltry attempts had been made to locate her. For example, no attempt was made to find her address through the Aboriginal Welfare Board.

I was immediately transferred to Blackburn South Cottages to be assessed for 'suitable adoptive placement'. When my Mother came for one of her visits, she found an empty cot. With the stroke of a pen, my Mother's Heart and Spirit had been shattered. Later, she was to describe this to me as one of the 'darkest days of her life'.

Repeated requests about my whereabouts were rejected. All her cries for help fell on deaf ears by a Government who had stolen her son, and who had decided 'they' knew what was best for this so-called part-Aboriginal boy.

In October 1967 I was placed with a family for adoption. This placement was a dismal failure, lasting only seven months. This family rejected me, and requested my removal, claiming in their words that I was unresponsive, dull, and that my so-called deficiencies were unacceptable. In the Medical Officer's report on my file there is a comment that Mrs A 'compared him unfavour-ably with her friends' children and finds his deficiencies an embarrassment, eg, at coffee parties'.

Upon removal, I was placed at the Gables Orphanage in Kew, where I was institutionalised for a further two years. Within this two years, I can clearly remember being withdrawn and frightened, and remember not talking to anyone for days on end.

I clearly remember being put in line-ups every fortnight, where prospective foster parents would view all the children. I was always left behind. I remember people coming to the Gables and taking me to their homes on weekends, but I would always be brought back. Apparently I wasn't quite the child they were looking for.

The Gables knew my dark complexion was a problem, constantly trying to reassure prospective foster parents that I could be taken as Southern European in origin. The following are some examples quoted from my file, which I received through Freedom of Information:

'Paul is dark-complexioned, dark hair and has brown eyes, He is part-Aboriginal, but does not look distinctly Aboriginal. In fact, he could be taken as Southern European.'

'In colouring, Paul could be fully Caucasian. His eyes and eye-lashes are dark and curly, his hair sleek and dark brown, but complexion is fair. Nose and eyes could identify him as an Aboriginal.'

'Paul has fine features, and is generally handsome looking. he has dark brown eyes and black curly hair. His skin is olive. He does not present as a part-Aboriginal lad, but could be just as easily identified as Maltese or Italian.'

In January 1970, I was again placed with a foster family, where I remained until I was seventeen. This family had four natural sons of their own. I was the only fostered child.

During this placement, I was acutely aware of my colour, and I knew I was different from the other members of their family. At no stage was I ever told of my Aboriginality, or my natural mother or father. When I'd say to my foster family, 'Why am I a different colour?', they would laugh at me, and would tell me to drink plenty of milk, 'and then you will look more like us'. The other sons would call me names such as 'their little Abo', and tease me.

At the time, I didn't know what this meant, but it did really hurt, and I'd run into the bedroom crying. They would threaten to hurt me if I told anyone they said these things.

My foster family made me attend the same primary and secondary school that their other children had all previously attended. Because of this, I was ridiculed and made fun of, by students and teachers. Everyone knew that I was different from the other family members and that I couldn't be their real brother, even though I'd been given the same surname as them. Often I would run out of class crying and would hide in the school grounds.

I had no identity. I always knew I was different. During my schooling years, I was forever asked what nationality I was, and I'd reply, 'I don't know'. I used to be laughed at, and was the object of jokes. I would constantly withdraw; my shadow was my best friend.

The foster family would punish me severely for the slightest thing they regarded as unacceptable or un-Christian-like behaviour, even if I didn't eat my dinner or tea. Sometimes I would be locked in my room for hours. Countless times the foster father would rain blows upon me with his favourite leather strap. He would continue until I wept uncontrollably, pleading for him to stop.

Towards the end of 1981 I was put under enormous pressure to sign papers consenting to the family officially adopting me. Because I refused to do this, I was told I was ungrateful for everything they had done for me, and to get out of their house and never come back.

Throughout these years—from five and a half months old to eighteen years of age, my Mother never gave up trying to locate me. She wrote many letters to the State Welfare Authorities, pleading with them to give her son back. Birthday and Christmas cards were sent care of the Welfare Department. All these letters were shelved. The State Welfare Department treated my Mother like dirt, and with utter contempt, as if she never existed. The Department rejected and scoffed at all my Mother's cries and pleas for help. They inflicted a terrible pain of Separation, Anguish and Grief upon a mother who only ever wanted her son back.

In May 1982, I was requested to attend at the Sunshine Welfare Offices, where they formerly discharged me from State wardship. It took the Senior Welfare Officer a mere twenty minutes to come clean, and tell me everything that my heart had always wanted to know. He conveyed to me in a matter-of-fact way that I was of 'Aboriginal descent', that I had a Natural mother, father, three brothers and a sister, who were alive.

He explained that his Department's position was only to protect me and, 'that is why you were not told these things before'. He placed in front of me 368 pages of my file, together with letters, photos and birthday cards. He informed me that my surname would change back to my Mother's maiden name.

The Welfare officer scribbled on a piece of paper my Mother's current address in case, in his words, I'd 'ever want to meet her'. I cried tears of Relief, Guilt and Anger. The official conclusion, on the very last page of my file, reads: 'Paul is a very intelligent, likeable boy, who has made remarkable progress, given the unfortunate treatment of his Mother by the department during his childhood'.

As I walked out of the Welfare Offices for the final time. I felt heartbroken. I felt my world had collapsed around me, and that my past was all a carefully constructed and premeditated lie. It was all false. I felt adrift, floating helplessly in a sea of Depression and Loneliness. I felt my life really didn't mean much any more. I knew there was only one person in my small world who I could turn to.

Early one morning as dawn began to break, I rang the doorbell and waited for an answer. I was almost about to turn away and get back in the car when my Mother opened the door. We instantly recognised each other and embraced.

With tears streaming down my Mother's face she said, 'I always knew that one day I would hold you gain, I never gave up. Please believe me, son, I never gave up'.

The next six years were the happiest, most cherished years of my life. My Mother and I picked up the shattered pieces of our lives, and put to one side the Pain, Bitterness and Unresolved Grief of the eighteen years of Forced Separation. My Mother hid her own terrible pain and hurt to help me come to terms with my own. She gave me Love, Strength, Culture, Identity, Family and Pride. She gave me everything that the State Welfare Department tried so desperately to prevent me from having.

On the 20th of November 1989, at the tender age of forty-five, my beautiful Mother died. Her last words to me were: 'I loved you then and I love you now. Always believe that, my boy'. I've lost my Mother, not once, but twice in a lifetime. I cherish the memories of my Mother who was so loving and compassionate. Her smile spoke a thousand words, her inner spiritual warmth radiated like the sun. She was a very special Elder who touched many lives. She did not possess a racist bone in her body. For the many, many people who respected my Mother, regardless of their colour or creed, she gave this respect twofold back. She was a living Angel, a tireless Community Worker, all her life, who cared for so many. My Mother never deserved the terrible pain and Anguish the State Welfare system of Victoria inflicted upon her. I was taken off my Mother simply because of our Aboriginality. To this very day, I still carry the pain and heartache of being taken away. Not only do I carry my pain, but also the pain of my Mother.

Not a day goes by without asking myself why, and pondering what could have been, and what should have been.

My Mother and I had eighteen years of love, bonding and happiness snatched away from us. To this very day, I often have bad days, where I feel isolated and alone. Often in the stillness of the night, I look at photos of my Mother and dream of what could have been, with tears of Love, Pride, Sadness and Hurt.

My relationship with my natural brothers and sisters is fractious after all these years. Although we try, we still don't really know each other; we're still like strangers. The same is with aunts and uncles. The happiness and childhood memories they share cannot be the same for me.

My Mother and Family's worlds were shattered by the State's and Commonwealth's despicable assimilation policies, and by the actions of the State Welfare Department who had the sheer audacity to decide they knew what was best for a 'part-Aboriginal boy'. Both my Mother and I were constantly lied to and manipulated—all done under the pretence that I was taken away for my own well-being.

As I tuck my children into bed at night, I look upon their innocent faces, and I cannot begin to imagine the terrible, terrible trauma and pain my Mother was put through, for no reason other than the fact that she was Aboriginal.

One may ask, how does one survive? Many Koori Brothers and Sisters don't. The pain is too much; the scars too deep. I was fortunate that my Mother was alive and waiting for me when I emerged from a system that almost destroyed me. My Mother taught me how to live with the pain as best as you can. Her determination, Pride and Spirit was her parting gift to me.

I cherish the handful of precious memories of a wonderful, devoted Mother who fought the system, took the blows, and never gave up, just so that she could embrace her first-born son one more time.

My final tribute to my beautiful Mother is in words that I often recite silently, words that often inspire me, when shades of darkness set in.

As years go by
A lonely heart

Although you've gone
We'll never part.
As days go by
A silent tear
Sweet memories of you
I hold so dear.
A Mother so strong, so caring and true
These are the memories I cherish of you.
Your Spirit you left
A part of me
Yes I can feel it more constantly.
It guides me through, day by day
The heartache I've felt, since you went away.
Once again, together we'll be
Only this time it will be for eternity.

2

Millicent's Story

THIS IS THE STORY of a girl who never saw her parents after the age of four, and who spent some of her life in Sister Kate's Home in Western Australia, some of it as a servant on a farm. It is a turbulent story of humiliation and rape, of physical and psychological abuse. The writer speaks of how she ate rat poison in an attempt to kill herself, and of an 'unrepairable scar of loneliness, mistrust, hatred and bitterness' that marks her heart. This is Confidential submission number 640.

AT THE AGE OF four, I was taken away from my family and placed in Sister Kate's Home, Western Australia, where I was kept as a ward of the State until I was eighteen years old. I was forbidden to see any of my family or know of their whereabouts. Five of us D. children were all taken and placed in different institutions in WA. The Protector of Aborigines and the Child Welfare Department in their 'Almighty Wisdom' said we would have a better life and future brought up as whitefellas away from our parents in a good religious environment. All they contributed to our upbringing and future was an unrepairable scar of loneliness, mistrust, hatred and bitterness. Fears that have been with me all of life. The empty, dark and lonely existence was so full of many hurtful and unforgivable events that I cannot escape from no matter how hard I try. Being deprived of the most cherished and valuable thing in life as an Aboriginal Child—love and family bonds. I would like to tell my story of my life in Sister Kate's Home, WA.

My name is Millicent D. I was born at Wonthella, WA, in 1945. My parents were CD and MP, both 'half-caste' Aborigines. I was one of seven children, our family lived in the sandhills at the back of the Geraldton Hospital. There was a lot of families living there happy and harmonious. It was like we were all part of one big happy family.

In 1949 the Protector of Aborigines with the Native Welfare Department visited the sandhill camps. All the families living there were to be moved to other campsites or to the Moore River Aboriginal Settlement. Because my parents were fair in complexion, the authorities decided us kids could pass as whitefellas. I was four years old and that was the last time I was to see my parents again. Because my sisters were older than me they were taken to the Government receiving home at Mount Lawley. My brother Kevin was taken to the boys' home in Kenwick. Colin and I were taken to the Sister Kate's Home. We were put in separate accommodation and hardly ever saw each other. I was so afraid and unhappy and didn't understand what was happening.

We were told Sundays was visiting day when parents and relatives came and spent the day. For Colin and I that was a patch of lies because our family were not allowed to visit. We spent each Sunday crying and comforting each other as we waited for our family. Each time it was the same—no-one came. That night we would cry ourselves to sleep and wonder why. We were too young to understand we were not allowed family visits.

A couple of years passed and I started primary school. It had been such a long time since I had seen my brother Colin. I was so helpless and alone. My brother had been taken away to the boys' home in Kenwick and now I was by myself. I became more withdrawn and shy and lived in a little world of my own hoping one day Mum would come and take me out of that dreadful place. As the years passed I realised I would never see my family again.

They told me that my family didn't care or want me and I had to forget them. They said it was very degrading to belong to an Aboriginal family and that I should be ashamed of myself, I was inferior to whitefellas. They tried to make us act like white kids but at the same time we had to give up our seat for a whitefella because an Aboriginal never sits down when a white person is present.

Then the religion began. We had church three times a day, before breakfast, lunchtime and after school. If we were naughty or got home from school late we had to kneel at the altar for hours and polish all the floors and brass in the church. We had religion rammed down our throats from hypocrites who didn't know the meaning of the word. We used to get whipped with a wet ironing cord and sometimes had to hold other children (naked) while they were whipped, and if we didn't hold them we got another whipping. To wake us up in the morning we were sprayed up the backside with an old-fashioned pump fly spray. If we complained we got more. Hurt and humiliation was a part of our everyday life and we had to learn to live with it.

Several more years passed and I still had no contact with my family, I didn't know what they looked like or how I could ever find them. By this time I was old enough to go to High School. This meant I didn't have to look after several of the younger kids as I had previously done, bathing, feeding and putting them on the potty and then off to bed, chopping wood before school and housework which all of us kids done and the housemothers sat back and collected wages—for doing nothing. My life was miserable, and I felt I was a nobody and things couldn't get any worse. But I was wrong.

The worst was yet to come.

While I was in first year high school I was sent out to work on a farm as a domestic. I thought it would be great to get away from the home for a while. At first it was. I was made welcome and treated with kindness. The four shillings I was paid went to the home. I wasn't allowed to keep it, I didn't care. I was never paid for the work I did at Sister Kate's so you don't miss what you didn't get, pocket money etc.

The first time I was sent to the farm for only a few weeks and then back to school. In the next holidays I had to go back. This time it was a terrifying experience, the man of the house used to come into my room at night and force me to have sex. I tried to fight him off but he was too strong.

When I returned to the home I was feeling so used and unwanted. I went to the Matron and told her what happened. She washed my mouth out with soap and boxed my ears and told me that awful things would happen to me if I told any of the other kids. I was scared and wanted to die. When the next school holidays came I begged not to be sent to that farm again. But they would not listen and said I had to.

I ran away from the home, I was going to try to find my family. It was impossible, I didn't even know where to go. The only thing was to go back. I got a good belting and had to kneel at the altar everyday after school for two weeks. Then I had to go back to that farm to work. The anguish and humiliation of being sent back was bad enough but the worse was yet to come.

This time I was raped, bashed and slashed with a razorblade on both of my arms and legs because I would not stop struggling and screaming. The farmer and one of his workers raped me several times. I wanted to die, I wanted my mother to take me home where I would be safe and wanted. Because I was bruised and in a state of shock I didn't have to do any work but wasn't allowed to leave the property.

When they returned me to the home I once again went to the Matron. I got a belting with a wet ironing cord, my mouth washed out with soap and put in a cottage by myself away from everyone so I couldn't talk to the other girls. They constantly told me that I was bad and a disgrace and that if anyone knew it would bring shame to Sister Kate's Home. They showed me no comfort which I desperately needed. I became more and more distant from everyone and tried to block everything out of my mind but couldn't. I ate rat poison to try and kill myself but became very sick and vomited. This meant another belting.

After several weeks of being kept away from everyone I was examined by a doctor who told Matron I was pregnant. Another belting, they blamed me for everything that happened. I didn't care what happened to me anymore and kept to myself. All I wanted now was to have my baby and get away as far as I could and try to find my family.

My daughter was born [in 1962] at King Edward Memorial Hospital. I was so happy, I had a beautiful baby girl of my own who I could love and cherish and have with me always.

But my dreams were soon crushed: the bastards took her from me and said she would be fostered out until I was old enough to look after her. They said when I left Sister Kate's I could have my baby back. I couldn't believe what was happening. My baby was taken away from me just as I was from my mother.

Once again I approached the Matron asking for the address of my family and address of the foster family who had my daughter. She said it was Government Policy not to give information about family and she could not help me. I then asked again about my baby girl and was told she did not know her whereabouts. In desperation I rang the King Edward Memorial Hospital. They said there was no record of me ever giving birth or of my daughter Toni. Then I wrote to the Native Welfare Department only to be told the same thing and that there were no records of the D family because all records were destroyed by fire.

I now had no other options but to find a job and somewhere to live. After working for a while I left Western Australia and moved to Adelaide to try to get my life together and put the past behind me. I was very alone, shy and not many friends and would break down over the simplest thing. Every time I saw a baby I used to wonder, could that be my little girl. I loved her and so desperately wanted her back. So in 1972 I returned to Western Australia and again searched for my family and child. I returned to see the Matron from Sister Kate's. This time she told me that my daughter was dead and it would be in my best interest to go back to South Australia and forget about my past and my family. I so wanted to find them, heartbroken I wandered the streets hoping for the impossible. I soon realised that I could come face to face with a family member and wouldn't even know.

Defeated I finally returned to Adelaide. In my heart I believed that one day everything would be alright and I would be reunited with my family. My baby was dead. (That's what I was told.) I didn't even get to hold her, kiss her and had no photographs, but her image would always be with me, and I would always love her. They couldn't take that away from me.

There is a happier postscript to Millicent's story. In January 1996, Millicent received an inquiry from the South Australian welfare authorities. She learned that a woman born in 1962 was searching for her birth mother. This woman was Toni, Millicent's daughter, and since then they have been reunited.

3

Eric's Story

THIS STORY WAS RELATED to the Inquiry by Eric's psychiatrist. It is Confidential submission number 64.

ERIC WAS REMOVED FROM parental care in 1957 when he was aged one.

[All of Eric's mother's children were eventually removed: one younger sister went to live with her grandmother; the other sister and a brother were fostered and later adopted. Eric and his older brother Kevin were placed in an orphanage in South Australia.]

Eric recalls being in an institution from the age of two and a half to six before he and Kevin were in the care of foster parents with whom Eric stayed until the age of eleven. Apparently he was then transferred to the care of an uncle and aunt. Kevin in the meantime became 'out of control' and Eric and Kevin were separated, with Kevin being sent to a boys' home while Eric remained in the care of his foster mother.

When Eric was sent to his uncle and aunt he stayed with them until about the age of thirteen or fifteen when he recalls running away because 'there was too much alcohol and violence.' He ran back to Adelaide and refused to return to the care of his uncle and aunt. He was then placed in a further foster placement which he remembers as being slightly better for the next three to four years, but left there at the age of seventeen.

At seventeen Eric became a street kid and once again he met up with his brother Kevin because it was the only family contact available to him at the time. He tells me that Kevin was mixing with criminals in Adelaide and that in 1972 Kevin just disappeared.

Eric never saw Kevin again, but Eric then returned to stay with his foster parents for a while at the age of eighteen or nineteen. He then recalls becoming an itinerant for a few years...When he returned to South Australia he was told that Kevin had died in the custody of police in Castlemaine whilst an inmate of the prison there.

Eric is brought easily to tears as he recalls the events of his life. In his own words, the most significant pain for him has been the loss of family and the separation from his own kin and his culture. When speaking of members of his family he feels a great emotional pain. In fact he doesn't believe that there is anyone left close to him. He feels as if he has been deprived of contact with his siblings by the separation at a young age, and he feels acutely the pain of his brother's death in custody.

The cumulative effects of these events for him are that he feels a great difficulty trusting anyone. He finds that when he turns to his own people their contact is unreliable. Whilst at some levels they are supportive, he doesn't feel able to trust the ongoing contact. His brothers have no long term training to be part of a family so that from time to time, out of their own aching, they will contact Eric, but they do not maintain contact. Eric finds these renewed contacts and separations from time to time painful because in a sense they give him a window onto what was available to him in the form of family support and what has been taken from him. In some ways he yearns to be closer to his family and in other ways he feels that whatever contact he has, always ends up being painful for him.

He tells me that he feels constantly afraid, with a sense of fear residing in his chest, that he is usually anxious and very jumpy and uptight. He feels angry with his own race, at the hurt that they have done to him, he feels that particularly the members of his own tribe exposed him to a life of alcohol, drugs and violence which has quickly turned against him.

He says looking within himself that he's a kind-hearted person, that it's not him to be angry or violent, but he certainly recalls a period of time in his life when it was the only behaviour that he felt able to use to protect himself...he feels that throughout his life he has had no anchor, no resting place, no relationship he could rely on or trust, and consequently he has shut people out of his life for the bigger proportion of his life. He tells me that the level of rejection he has experienced hurts him immensely. In fact he says, 'It tears me apart'. He tries very hard not to think about too much from the past because it hurts too much, but he finds all the anger and the hurt, the humiliations, the beatings, the rejection of the past, from time to time boil up in him and overflow, expressing themselves in verbal abuse of [de facto] and in violent outbursts.

Eric often relates feelings of fear. He remembers from his childhood feelings of intense fear. He has related to me incidents with his foster mother whom he was with from the age of six to eleven.

He specifies particular details of physical cruelty and physical assault as well as emotional deprivation and punishment that would, in this age, be perceived as cruel in the extreme.

Eric describes to me how, throughout his childhood, he would wet himself and how he had a problem with bed-wetting, but he also would receive punishment for these problems. He lived in fear of his foster mother. When he was taken away from her and brought again before the welfare authorities he was too afraid to tell them what had happened to him. At that stage he and his brother Kevin were separated and Eric found that separation extremely painful because he was too frightened to be left alone with that foster mother.

One of the effects that Eric identifies in himself is that, because of the violence in his past, when he himself becomes angry or confused, he feels the anger, the rage and violence welling up within him. He tells me: 'I could have done myself in years ago, but something kept me going'.

In the light of the research findings, Eric's experiences of separation were both highly traumatic for him and also occurred at an age when he would have been most vulnerable to serious disturbance.

For Eric too the separation involved a disruption to his cultural and racial identity.

It is apparent to me that a fundamental diagnosis of Post-Traumatic Stress Disorder is fitting. Eric's symptomatology is obviously severe and chronic. In addition, it is clear that he deals with many deep emotional wounds that do not clearly fit [this] diagnostic classification. His deep sense of loss and abandonment, his sense of alienation, and his gross sense of betrayal and mistrust are normal responses to a tragic life history. Having said this, it is also apparent that he deals from time to time with Major Depressive Episodes.

4

Evie's Story

THIS STORY OUTLINES four generations of pain and separation, exposing the devastation caused to the lives and the spirits of the Indigenous people. Evie looks back at the lives of her mother and her grandmother. In them she traces the same wrongs as she experienced herself, and sees her own children taken from her, alienated and still suffering. 'You leave the baby here', they said. 'You leave the baby here'. This is Confidential evidence number 557.

MY GRANDMOTHER WAS TAKEN from up Tennant Creek. What gave them the right to just go and take them? They brought her down to The Bungalow at Alice Springs. Then she had Uncle Billy and my Mum to an Aboriginal Protection Officer. She had no say in that from what I can gather. And then from there they sent her out to Hermannsburg—because you know, she was only fourteen when she had Uncle Billy, fifteen when she had Mum. When she was fifteen and a half they took her to Hermannsburg and married her to an Aranda man. That's a no-no.

And then from there, when Mum was three they ended up taking Mum from Hermannsburg, putting her in The Bungalow until she was eleven. And then they sent her to Mulgoa mission in New South Wales. And there they sent her to Carlingford Girls'

Home to be a maid. She couldn't get back to the Territory and she'd had a little baby.

Agnes, my sister, and I have met him [their older brother]. We met him when he was thirty-five. He's now forty-two so that's not far away. Mum had him when she was working but she doesn't know what happened to her money. When she kept asking for her money so she could pay her fare back to Alice Springs they wouldn't give her any.

I've got paperwork on her from the Archives in New South Wales. There's letters—stacks of 'em—between the Aboriginal Protection Board, New South Wales, and the Northern Territory. All on my mother. They were fighting about which jurisdiction she was in—New South Wales, yet she was a kid from the Northern Territory. So one State was saying we're not paying because she's New South Wales. They should pay.

In the end New South Wales said to Mum, 'We'll pay your fare back on the condition that because you haven't got a husband, and you've got a baby, you leave the baby here'. So she left her baby behind and came back to the Territory.

And then she had me and then my brother and another two brothers and a sister and we were all taken away as soon as we were born. Two of them were put in Retta Dixon and by the time they were eighteen months old they were sent down south and adopted. She had two kids, like they were fifteen months apart, but as soon as they turned eighteen months old they were sent down south and adopted out.

One of them came back in 1992. He just has that many problems. The others—we don't know where they are. So it's like we've still got a broken family.

I was taken away in 1950 when I was six hours old from the hospital and put into Retta Dixon until I was two months old and then sent to Garden Point. I lived in Garden Point until 1964. And from Garden Point, Tennant Creek, Hermannsburg. While in Garden Point I always say that some of it was the happiest time of my life; others it was the saddest time of my life. The happiest time was, 'Yippee! all these other kids there'. You know, you got to play with them every day. The saddest times were the abuse. Not only physical abuse, the sexual abuse by the priests over there. They were the saddest because if you were to tell anyone, well, the priests threatened that they would actually come and get you.

Everyone could see what they were doing but were told to keep quiet. And just every day you used to get hidings with the stock-whip. Doesn't matter what you did wrong, you'd get a hiding with the stock-whip. If you didn't want to go to church, well you got slapped about the head. We had to go to church three times a day. I was actually relieved to leave the Island.

Q: Did any girls get pregnant at Garden Point when you were there?

I remember one and they actually took her off the Island. And when I ask everyone, like even now when I ask people about her, they don't know what happened to her. All they remember is her being put on the helicopter and flown out and I've never heard about her, about her name or anything about her anymore. They remember her, but I don't know what happened to her.

Q; Who was the Father?

The Priest. The same bastards who...

Q: How do people know that?

Well, the reason they know is, Sister A, poor thing, who's dead—I know she was upset because that priest had that young girl living in his place. He used to come and get her out of the dormitory every night. He used to sneak in about half past twelve, one o'clock in the morning and take her. We'd get up in the morning and she'd be just coming in the door.

All the girls slept in one dormitory. All the boys slept in the other. And we couldn't lock the dormitory from the inside—it

had a chain through and padlock outside, so there was only the
nuns or priest who could get in there. I know he used to come
and get her because I was three beds up from her.

There was another priest, but he's dead. The rest of the mob
that were on the Island are all dead. He's the only one that's
kicking and he should have been the one that's bloody dead for
what he did. He not only did it to girls, he did it to boys as well.
There was six of 'em involved. Nuns were assaulting the young
fellas as well as the priest assaulting the young fellas and the girls.

There were four priests and two nuns involved. We were in
their care. That fella's still walking around. He's now got charge
of other kids.

By 1977 I had three children. My oldest was three years old
then. I had another one that was twelve months and another that
was two months old. All those kids were taken off me. The reason
behind that was, well, I'd asked my girlfriend and so-called sister-
in-law if she could look after my kids. She wouldn't look after my
daughter because my daughter's black. So, she said she'd take the
two boys and that was fine. And while I was in hospital for three
months—that's the only reason I had asked them to take 'em
'cause I was going to hospital because I had septicaemia.

I couldn't get my kids back when I came out of hospital. And
I fought the welfare system for ten years and still couldn't get 'em.
I gave up after ten years. Once I gave up I found out that while I
was in hospital, my sister-in-law wanted to go overseas with my
two boys 'cause her husband was being posted there for twelve
months from foreign affairs. And I know she brought some papers
in for me to sign while I was in hospital and she said they were just
papers for their passports. Stupid me, being sick and what-have-
you didn't ask questions—I signed 'em and found out too late
they were adoption papers. I had thirty days to revoke any orders
that I'd signed.

And with my daughter, well she came back in '88 but things
aren't working out there. She blames me for everything that went

wrong. She's got this hate about her—doesn't want to know. The two boys know where I am but turned around and said to us, 'You're not our mother—we know who our real mother is'.

So every day of your bloody life you just get hurt all the time.

5

The Story of Penny and Murray

PENNY AND MURRAY ARE sister and brother. They came from Palm Island, and they tell their story together. It is particularly apt and poignant that this brother and sister speak together, since the authorities treated their family with what Penny describes as a 'split the litter' approach. The children were scattered. For ten years they did not see their mother, after she transgressed by visiting them at the school fence. Their letters to her were never answered, probably never sent. And their skin was too dark for them to be taken in by white foster families. Some of the documents about them from the Queensland State Children's Department in Townsville are quoted in the story which is from Confidential submissions numbers 191 and 776.

PENNY:
IN 1958, WHILST OUR family, [Penny aged ten, her brother Trevor eleven, Murray seven, sister Judy six and baby Olive was five or six weeks old, their mother and step-father] were all resident at a house situated in Cairns, my mother's capacity to look after her children in a fit and proper manner became the subject of challenge within the Cairns District Children's Court. This action was initiated by Sergeant Syd Wellings, then attached to the nearby Edmonton Police Station.

At the end of those proceedings, it was determined by the court that we be made wards of the State and as such we were to be placed under the care and protection of the Queensland State Children's Department [shared with the Department of Native Affairs]. We were transferred via train to the State Children's Orphanage at Townsville.

It was as though someone had turned the lights out—a regimented existence replacing our childhood innocence and frolics —the sheer snugness, love, togetherness, safety and comfort of four of us sleeping in one double bed—family! Strange how the bureaucracy adopt the materialistic yardstick when measuring poverty/deprivation/neglect.

[Baby] Olive was taken elsewhere—Mr L [Children's Department official] telling me several days later that she was admitted to the Townsville General Hospital where she had died from meningitis. In 1984, assisted by Link-Up [Queensland], my sister Judy discovered that Olive had not died in 1956 but rather had been fostered. Her name was changed. Judy and Trevor were able to have a reunion with Olive in Brisbane during Christmas of 1984. I was reunited with Olive sometime during 1985 and Murray had his first meeting with Olive two months ago.

MURRAY:
I DO REMEMBER MY mother showing up for visits, supervised visits. We used to get excited. I just wanted her to take us away from there. Then the visits suddenly stopped. I'm told the authorities stopped them because she had a destabilising effect on us.

That didn't deter my mother. She used to come to the school ground to visit us over the fence. The authorities found out about those visits. They had to send us to a place where she couldn't get to us. To send us anywhere on mainland Queensland, she would have just followed—so they sent us to the one place where she can't follow: Palm Island Aboriginal Settlement. By our mother visiting us illegally at that school ground she unknowingly sealed our fate. I wasn't to see my mother again for ten nightmare years.

I remember when I learnt to write letters, I wrote to my mother furiously pleading with her to come and take us off that island. I wrote to her for years, I got no reply then I realised that she was never coming for us; that she didn't want us. That's when I began to hate her. Now I doubt if any of my letters ever got off that island or that any letters she wrote me ever stood a chance of me receiving them.

Penny:

Early in 1959, under a 'split the litter' approach, the State Children's Department bureaucracy sanctioned Judy's being fostered to a European family resident in Townsville, Trevor's being 'shipped off' or 'deported' to Palm Island Aboriginal Settlement.

Trevor's file reveals he was transferred to Palm Island because he was 'a great trouble' to the Orphanage. 'He has given us no serious trouble, although inclined to be somewhat disobedient at times. We find that physical punishment has little or no effect on him and that the best way to punish him is by depriving him of privileges'.

Murray and myself were to follow Trevor some time later. I recall our being driven to the landing at Hayles Wharf at 4.30–5.00 am, given two small ports [suitcases] and being told to 'catch that boat to Palm Island over there' then leaving us there. Bewilderment, scared, where was Palm Island? What was Palm Island? Why were we going there?

A document from the State Children's Department, Townsville to the Superintendent, Palm Island in October 1958 states:

As you will realize, it is almost impossible to find suitable Foster Homes for such children and they do not fit in very well with white children in institutions, such as are conducted by this Department. It would be greatly appreciated if you could advise whether it would be possible to admit all, or some of these children to Palm Island.

And another document from the same source in June 1960 says: 'These two children have been in our home in Townsville for more than two years, and in view of their very dark colouring, have not been assimilated in the white race. Every effort has been made to place them in a foster home without success because of their colour'.

PENNY:

I can't remember much about when or why it was decided that Murray and I should leave the Orphanage and be sent to Palm Island—just know that I came home from school one afternoon and walked in on two other girls. They were both crying and then told me that Murray and I were going to be sent to Palm Island, it was where Trevor had been sent.

Prior to that information—didn't know what the hell had happened to Trevor, Matron told me that he was going on a picnic, he never came back on that day and we never saw him again until we were reunited with Trevor on Palm Island some time later.

After a while you just give up asking and learn acceptance of situations even though you don't fully understand the whys and wherefores.

'We will notify some responsible person on the boat as to the circumstances concerning these children and no doubt you will arrange to have them met on arrival at Palm Island', says a letter from the State Children's Department, Townsville to the Superintendent, Palm Island in July 1960.

PENNY:

Upon arrival at Palm Island we were lost, we went to the Police Station—the sergeant advised as we were white children that we must have caught the wrong boat and maybe should have been on the one that went to Magnetic Island. He also said that no one was allowed onto Palm Island without the Superintendent's permission. I informed the sergeant that my brother Trevor was already on Palm Island. After meeting with Trevor over at the school—we were taken into the Superintendent's office [Mr B] and he said that we shouldn't have been sent to the Island, that there must have been some mistake. He said that he would have to look into matters and in the meantime that I would be taken to the young girls' dormitory and that Murray would be with Trevor in the boys' home. Mr B lost the battle to have us returned to the Oprhanage at Townsville.

MURRAY:

At that time Palm Island was regarded by many, both black and white as nothing more than an Aboriginal Penal Colony. Our only crime was coming from a broken home. Palm Island was ruled with an iron fist by a White administration headed by a Superintendent whose every word was law which was brutally enforced by Aboriginal Policemen who were nothing more than a group of thugs and criminals in uniform.

If I were to write a book of my childhood experiences, I would write of my arrival as an eight-year-old boy. I would write of how I was spat on by Aboriginal adults, all complete strangers. Of being called a little White bastard and names much too vile to mention. It didn't matter to those people that I was just a kid. The colour of my skin and eyes were enough to warrant their hostile attentions.

I would write of regular beatings and of being locked in a cell on many occasions on the whim of a Black Woman who was a female guardian of that home.

I would tell of a White headmaster belting the living daylights out of me because he overheard me tell a Black classmate not to crawl to White teachers; of how I felt his hot stinking breath on my face as he screamed, 'How dare I say such a thing being White myself'.

That island was seething with hatred for the White Man and his System so why in God's name were three fair skinned children condemned to such a place?

Eventually, my siblings and I got off that terrible place. Towards the end of our unpleasant stay on that island the populace finally accepted us. The harsh treatment subsided and eventually ceased as did the swearing and suspicious looks. Today many people from that island are our closest and dearest friends. But I'll never go back to visit, it holds too many painful memories for me.

PENNY:

Judy had the resources to seek psychiatric care. Murray's got psychiatric care. Trevor's still under psychiatric care and been diagnosed as paranoid schizophrenic. His psychiatrist says he attributes all the things that happened to him in his childhood to bring him to that state he is in today. Sometimes he gets suicidal. He rings up and wants to kill himself. And I say, 'Don't let your life pass into nothingness'.

People probably see on the surface that we've led successful lives. But that's on the surface. Nobody knows that Trevor, until six years ago, has never been out of a job in his life, owns his own home, got his own car. They look at that and say, 'He's achieved the great Australian dream'. And they don't look behind that. Is that what it's all about? They look at us and say, 'Well, assimilation worked with those buggers'. They see our lives as a success.

6

Murray's Journal

THIS PIECE WAS NOT included in *Bringing Them Home*. It is a further insight into Murray's life, and into the meaning of racial issues for people of mixed race. It is a testament to the struggle Indigenous people have in making themselves heard.

ALLOW ME TO EXTEND to you the reader, through this journal, an invitation to accompany me on a journey back through the darkest years of my life. Join me as I search for what was taken from me, for that which was denied me. Join me in my search for something I have lost. Let us begin.

I wasted a lifetime drinking and drifting from place to place, an aimless and purposeless life. Why did I drink? I can honestly say I didn't know. I never really enjoyed it. I used to get into a lot of fights due to drinking and most of the time it was over a racial issue.

Then my whole life was upended about two years ago when I suffered renal failure. My drinking career came to an abrupt halt, due to the damage done to my kidneys. It would have been suicide for me to continue drinking.

Eighteen months further down the track, I wrote letters to the 'Letters to the Editor' column of a northern paper for a black mate of mine, Joe. Always in response to letters attacking the black race, I wrote about five letters for Joe. Then I had to write letters myself in response to a vile letter which was published in that paper. The letter to which I responded said in part that 'anyone with less Aboriginal blood than a half-caste' was not an Aboriginal. That was pre-Whitlam days as that racist had it. He further stated in his letter that he found light-skinned blacks amusing.

I don't come anywhere near being half-cast, I have green eyes and fair skin (for a black) and I certainly don't find anything amusing about me or what happened in my life. So I wrote a reply to that reptile's letter. I took his letter apart word by word, but for obvious reasons the editor of the paper didn't publish my letter. There was a big question in my response that asked, what was a non-Aboriginal eight-year-old boy doing in an Aboriginal settlement? A place that was regarded by many a black penal colony.

As a result of writing my letter, and the stress and anxiety it put me through, I ended up in the emergency department of a hospital at four in the morning. Hello, post-traumatic stress disorder: bad things that happened to me in the past started to come back to me.

As the years of my childhood went by a son's love for his mother turned to hatred that destroys any feeling of love for anyone. I must have been twelve or thirteen years old. I always had trouble remembering my age when I was a young bloke, I've never had a birthday in my life. Normal people use birthdays as a milepost as they travel down the highway of life, and they can look back and recall where they were at such and such an age. To me time and life were meaningless. Now I have to race against time to make something of what's left of my life.

I was the last to leave the island. After about eighteen years drifting on the mainland, my older sister led me back to see my mother, I didn't want to have anything to do with her. So I went more out of curiosity than anything else. When we met we were both strangers, something was lost, taken, stolen. The gap was too wide to be bridged.

I spent a few weeks with her, to try to get to know her again but it wasn't to be. I used to catch her looking at me in sad sort of a way many times. Sometimes I woke up suddenly to see her sitting there watching me with that sad look. When I left that woman, that I once called Mum as a little boy, I knew in my heart that I was never to see her again, ever. I was eighteen years old and I was dead right.

My mother spent the final years of her life with my older sister. Towards the end her mind went, she was an invalid. She wasn't stark raving mad, she just needed constant supervision so she wouldn't wander off. My mother died on the first day of January 1977, a tormented and broken woman. She was fifty-seven years old.

My mate, Joe, said to me that the worst thing that could ever happen to any woman, black or white, was to have her children taken from her. I can see a lot clearer now. I was too blind to see before.

I wept silent bitter tears at my mother's funeral. I wept for the five children, I wept for a mother I never knew, I wept for the question that I never had the courage to ask her when she was alive: 'Did you ever love me, even just a little, in the short time we were together?' I left my mother's graveside eighteen months ago, I never went back. I think the time has come for me to return soon, after all she is my mother and who am I to judge so harshly. Whatever crimes were committed we didn't deserve life sentences, a sentence I still serve today. Thirty-eight years on. When I lie awake at night and the dark memories come clouding in on me, I keep seeing a scene in my mind of a woman crying at the end of my bed. I can't see her face in the darkness, is it her? My sister seems to think so, she said our mother cried a lot when we were young. Is it a memory trying to break through.

About ten years after my mother's death, her father, my grandfather, died. He was laid to rest on the west side of Cape York Peninsula, the ancestral home of his mother, my great-grandmother. It was asked at his funeral: 'Where is his daughter? Why isn't she here at her father's burial and whatever happened to her and her children?'

I guess they will never know.

Well, dear reader and travelling companion, our journey is almost at an end. Perhaps one day in the future I'll take you through my life again. The final chapters have yet to be written. Before we part company to continue our separate journeys through life, I want you to know that I did find something. Perhaps I did not lose it at all, perhaps it lay buried under a lifetime of bad memories. What I found was forgiveness and a love for my mother they took away from me.

7

Greg's Story

IN ONE CHILLING PHRASE Greg begins the story of his removal from his family and way of life: 'there was a knock at the door'. His description of how he went from Cape Barren Island in Bass Strait to Tasmania reads like a kidnapping. In spite of all the sadness and bitterness, Greg speaks with affection of his foster family in Hobart. This story is Confidential evidence number 384.

I WAS BORN ON Cape Barren. At the time I was taken the family comprised mum, my sister and (my two brothers). And of course there was my grandmother and all the other various relatives. We were only a fairly small isolated community and we all grew up there in what I considered to be a very peaceful, loving community. I recall spending most of my growing up on the Island actually living in the home of my grandmother and grandfather. The other children were living with mum in other places.

Until the time I was taken I had not been away from the Island, other than our annual trips from Cape Barren across to Lady Baron during the mutton bird season.

The circumstances of my being taken, as I recollect, were that I went off to school in the morning and I was sitting in the classroom and there was only one room where all the children were assembled and there was a knock at the door, which the schoolmaster answered. After a conversation he had with somebody at the door, he came to get me. He took me by the hand and took me to the door. I was physically grabbed by a male person at the door, I was taken to a motorbike and held by the officer and driven to the airstrip and flown off the Island. I was taken from Cape Barren in October 1959 [aged twelve].

I had no knowledge [I was going to be taken]. I was not even able to see my grandmother [and I had] just the clothes I had on my back, such as they were. I never saw mum again.

To all intents and purposes, I guess my grandmother was looked upon as my mother in some respects because of my association with her, and when I was taken there are actual letters on my file that indicate that she was so affected by the circumstances of my being removed from the Island that she was hospitalised, and was fretting and generally her health went on her. A nursing sister on the Island had my grandmother in hospital and she was in fact writing letters to the Welfare Department to find out, you know, how I was getting on and that sort of thing, and asking if I could go back to the Island for holidays. That was refused. My grandmother was removed from the Island and placed in an aged-care hospital, and I was taken to see her and when I did she had basically lost her mind and she did not know who I was.

It is fairly evident from reading my welfare file that [the teacher] was the eyes and ears of the Welfare Department and that he was obviously sending reports back to them about the conditions on the Island.

There is a consent form on [my] file that mum signed and it did include [my sister and my two brothers]— and their names were crossed out and mine was left. I do not know whether it was because I was at the top or not. I might add that most people that I have spoken to said that mum, whilst she could read her name, could not read or write, and obviously would not have understood the implications of what she was signing. [It] has been witnessed by the schoolmaster.

I was flown off the Island and...I was flown to where the small planes land at Launceston. I was eventually placed with some people in Launceston. I have some recollection of going to school at some stage. I noted from my file that I was transported to Hobart in 1960—my recollection of that was being put into a semitrailer and picked up on the side of the road by some welfare officers down there. I was placed with some people in [Hobart], and I guess, fortunately for me, I could not have been in better hands because I still maintain a relationship with them; they look on me as their son. They had one daughter but Mrs— used to care for other foster children and the house was full of other non-Aboriginal children.

I had always wanted to return to the Island but I could never bring myself to hopping on a plane and returning. [It was] thirty years before I went back. [The night I returned] I could not settle. I think I had a cup of tea and I decided I would go in a different direction and I walked around the sand spit and—I do not know, something just made me turn around and look back and I looked to the school and—I just looked back to where we used to live as kids. My whole life flashed before me and I just collapsed in the sand and started crying...And when I composed myself as best I could I just sort of reflected on things and my whole life was just racing through my mind and I guess I just wanted to be part of a family that I never had. I just wanted to be with my mum and my grandmother and my brother and sisters.

The consent form signed by Greg's mother states the reason for his removal: 'I am a widow, in poor health'. After Greg was taken his mother had another daughter but Greg was not aware of her existence until 1994. One of Greg's brothers states that after Greg went their mother 'was in total despair'. They lived in conditions of extreme poverty in 'a run down shanty'. One afternoon their mother went drinking and suffered a fatal accident. Later police came to collect the children and flew them to Launceston. The boys were fostered together but each of the girls went to a different family. The first time the five children were all together was in 1995.

8

Jennifer's Story

THE CHILDREN OF JENNIFER'S family have been stolen over and over again throughout three generations, beginning early this century.

In this story of the missions and of life with white families, there are references to physical abuse and murder, and to sexual abuse of young Indigenous girls, including the chilling sentence: 'Some girls just disappeared never to be seen or heard of again'. The story ends on a note of sad and endless puzzlement: 'I still can't see why we were taken away from our home'. This story is Confidential submission number 437.

MY GRANDMOTHER, REBECCA, WAS born around 1890. She lived with her tribal people, parents and relations around the Kempsey area. Rebecca was the youngest of a big family. One day some religious people came, they thought she was a pretty little girl. She was a full-blood Aborigine about five years old. Anyway those people took her to live with them.

Rebecca could not have been looked after too well. At the age of fourteen she gave birth to my mother Grace and later on Esther, Violet and May. She married my grandfather Laurie, and at the age of twenty-three she died from TB.

Grandfather took the four girls to live with their Aunty and

Uncle on their mother's side. Grandfather worked and supported the four girls.

Mum said in those days the aboriginals did not drink. She often recalled going to the river and her Uncle spearing fish and diving for cobbler. Mum had eaten kangaroo, koala bear, turtles and porcupine. She knew which berries were edible, we were shown by her how to dig for yams and how to find witchetty grubs. My mother also spoke in several aboriginal languages she knew as a small girl. The aboriginals had very strict laws and were decent people. They were kind and had respectable morals. Even though the girls fretted for their mother they felt secure with their own people.

Years later, Grandfather told my mother a policeman came to his work with papers to sign. The girls were to be placed in Cootamundra Home where they would be trained to get a job when they grew up. If Grandfather didn't sign the papers he would go to jail and never come out, this was around 1915.

My grandfather was told he was to take the four girls by boat to Sydney. The girls just cried and cried and the relations were wailing, just like they did when Granny Rebecca had died.

In Sydney my mother and Esther were sent by coach to Cootamundra. Violet and May were sent to the babies' home at Rockdale. Grace and Esther never saw their sister Violet again. She died at Waterfall Hospital within two years from TB. My mother was to wait twenty years before she was to see her baby sister May again.

Cootamundra in those days was very strict and cruel. The home was overcrowded. Girls were coming and going all the time. The girls were taught reading, writing and arithmetic. All the girls had to learn to scrub, launder and cook.

Mum remembered once a girl who did not move too quick. She was tied to the old bell post and belted continuously. She died that night, still tied to the post, no girl ever knew what happened to the body or where she was buried.

Aunty Esther was a big girl for her age, so she was sent out as a cook to work at twelve years of age. Mum being of smaller build was sent out as children's nurse at fourteen. She had responsibility for four young children; one only a baby for twenty-four hours a day. Mum said they used to put girls' ages up if they were big for their age and send them out to work on properties. Some girls were belted and sexually abused by their masters and sent to the missions to have their babies. Some girls just disappeared, never to be seen or heard of again.

Eventually, after several years, Mum was sent to Rose Bay to work. Whilst in Sydney she met her sister Esther who was working in the Chatswood area. As far as I know, neither Mum or Aunt Esther ever got paid for those hard working years under the Board.

My mother often recalled the joyous time Aunty May came to Kempsey to see her sisters and father. The three young women hugged one another and cried with happiness and sadness for their sister and their mother.

Early one morning in November 1952, the manager from Burnt Bridge Mission came to our home with a policeman. I could hear him saying to Mum, 'I am taking the two girls and placing them in Cootamundra Home'. My father was saying, 'What right have you?' The manager said he can do what he likes, they said my father had a bad character (I presume they said this as my father associated with aboriginal people). They would not let us kiss our father goodbye. I will never forget the sad look on his face. He was unwell and he worked very hard all his life as a timbercutter. That was the last time I saw my father, he died within two years.

We were taken to the manager's house at Burnt Bridge. Next morning we were in court. I remember the judge saying, 'These girls don't look neglected to me'. The manager was saying all sorts of things. He wanted us placed in Cootamundra Home. So we were sent away not knowing that it would be five years before we came back to Kempsey again.

Mum used to write to us every week. Sometimes it would be two months before we received the letters, of course they were opened and read first. Sometimes parts would be torn out of the letters by Matron or whoever was in charge.

Cootamundra was so different from the North Coast, it was cold and dry. I missed the tall timbers and all the time I was away there was this loneliness inside of me. I had often thought of running away but Kate was there and I was told to always look after her. I had just turned eleven and Kate was still only seven. I often think now of Cootamundra as a sad place, I think of thousands of girls who went through that home, some girls that knew what family love was and others that never knew; they were taken away as babies.

Some of the staff were cruel to the girls. Punishment was caning or belting and being locked in the box-room or the old morgue. Matron had her pets and so did some of the staff. I look back now and see we were all herded together like sheep and each had to defend themselves and if you didn't you would be picked on by somebody that didn't like you, your life would be made a misery. I cannot say from my memories Cootamundra was a happy place. In the home on Sundays we often went to two different churches, hymns every Sunday night. The Seventh Day Adventist and Salvation Army came through the week. With all the different religions it was very confusing to find out my own personal and religious beliefs throughout my life.

My mother sent us a new outfit every change of season, we only received one parcel. The matron kept our clothes and distributed them to her pets. In winter it was icy cold and for the first time in my life I didn't have socks to wear to school.

One day the matron called me to her office. She said it was decided by the Board that Kate and myself were to go and live with a lady in a private house. The Board thought we were too 'white' for the home. We were to be used as an experiment and if everything worked out well, more girls would be sent later on. We travelled all day long. We didn't know what place we were going to, all I knew was we were going further and further away from home. Late afternoon we stopped at this house in Narromine. There lived Mrs S, her son and at weekends her husband Lionel.

The twenty months Kate and I spent at Narromine were honestly the worst time of my childhood life. I often thought I would not survive long enough ever to see my mother again.

The Scottish woman hated me because I would not call her 'Mum'. She told everyone I was bad. She made us stay up late sewing, knitting and darning that pillowcase full of endless socks. Often we weren't allowed to go to bed till after 11 pm. I was always late for school, the headmaster used to greet me with, 'Good afternoon, Jennifer'. Mrs S did not allow me to do home-work, therefore my schoolwork suffered and myself—a nervous wreck.

When I was thirteen years old Mrs S called this middle-aged male doctor to the house and said she wanted an internal examination of me. That was terribly shameful for me, I will not say anymore. During the time [with her] I was belted naked repeatedly, whenever she had the urge. She was quite mad. I had to cook, clean, attend to her customers' laundry. I was used and humiliated. The Board knew she was refused anymore white children yet they sent us there.

Near the end of our stay she got Mr F from Dubbo to visit. She tried to have me put in Parramatta Girls' Home. By this time I knew other people had complained to the Board. Mr F asked me if I wanted to go to a white home or back to Cootamundra. So a couple of days later we were back in the home. It was hard to believe we had gotten away from that woman.

It wasn't long after we were back at the home and Matron called me to her office. She wanted to know what had happened at Narromine. I told her everything. She said the experiment did not work and she would write to the Board for fear they would send more girls out. It did not do any good though because more than half the girls were fostered out over the next three years. Some of the girls were sexually abused, belted and called names by their foster parents. Of course the brainwashing continued about Aboriginals being lazy, dirty and of low intelligence going nowhere.

In December 1957 our mother finally got us home. She was the first Aboriginal to move into a Commission house. My mother died four years later, she suffered high blood pressure, she was fifty-four years old. It was fight all the way to survive because she was born an Aboriginal.

I still can't see why we were taken away from our home. We were not neglected, we wore nice clothes, we were not starving. Our father worked hard and provided for us and we came from a very close and loving family.

I feel our childhood has been taken away from us and it has left a big hole in our lives.

9

John's Story

JOHN'S STORY IS BLEAK and heartbreaking. It is told in plain and vivid detail—the image of small boys being herded in behind the iron gates of the orphanage, their heads shaved their numbers stamped on their clothes, their little suitcases containing only their Bibles being cast into the flames. And after that they are beaten and sodomised and turned against each other. Prisoners. John says he will always be a prisoner as long as his records remain in the archives. This is Confidential evidence number 436.

WE DIDN'T HAVE A clue where we came from. We thought the Sisters were our parents. They didn't tell anybody—any of the kids—where they came from. Babies were coming in nearly every day. Some kids came in at two, three, four days old, not months but days. They were just placed in the home and it was run by Christian women and all the kids thought it was one big family. We didn't know what it meant by 'parents' 'cause we didn't have parents and we thought those women were our mothers.

I was definitely not told that I was Aboriginal. What the Sisters told us was that we had to be white. It was drummed into our heads that we were white. It didn't matter what shade you were. We thought we were white. They said you can't talk to any of them coloured people because you're white.

I can't remember anyone from the welfare coming there. If they did I can't remember…we hardly saw any visitors whatsoever. None of the other kids had visits from their parents. No visits from family. The worst part is, we didn't know we had a family.

When you got to a certain age, like I got to ten years old…they just told us were were going on a train trip…We all lined up with our little ports [school cases] with a bible inside. That's all that was in the ports, see. We really treasured that, we thought it was a good thing that we had something…the old man from La Perouse took us from Sydney, well actually from Bomaderry to Kinchela Boys' Home. That's when our problems really started, you know!

This is where we learned that we weren't white. First of all they took you in through these iron gates and took our little ports off us. Stick it in the fire with your little bible inside. They took us around to a room and shaved our hair off…They gave you your clothes and stamped a number on them…They never called you by your name; they called you by your number. That number was stamped on everything.

If we answered an attendant back we were 'sent up the line'. Now I don't know if you can imagine, seventy-nine boys punching the hell out of you, just knuckling you. Even your brother, your cousin.

They had to, if they didn't do it, they were sent up the line. When the boys who had broken ribs or broken noses—they'd have to pick you up and carry you right through to the last bloke. Now that didn't happen once, that happened every day.

Before I went to Kinchela, they used to use the cat-o-nine-tails on the boys instead of being sent up the line. This was in the thirties and early forties.

Kinchela was a place where they thought you were animals. You know it was like a place where they go around and kick us like a dog…It was just like a prison. Truthfully, there were boys having sex with boys…But these other dirty mongrels didn't care. We had a manager who was sent to prison because he was doing it to a lot of the boys, sexual abuse. Nothing was done. There was a pommie bloke that was doing it. These attendants—if the boys told them, they wouldn't even listen. It just happened...I don't like talking about it.

We never went into town...the school was in the home...all we did was work, work, work. Every six months you were dressed up. Oh mate! You were done up beautiful—white shirt. The welfare used to come up from Bridge Street, the main bloke, the superintendent to check the home out—every six months.

We were prisoners from when we were born...The girls who went to Cootamundra and the boys who went to Kinchela—we were all prisoners. Even today they have our file number so we're still prisoners you know. And we'll always be prisoners while our files are in archives.

10

Carol's Story

CAROL'S GRANDMOTHER WAS REMOVED to Beagle Bay Mission at the age of ten. She and her husband had ten children. When her husband was transferred to the Derby leprosarium, their children were placed in the Beagle Bay dormitories. Carol's mother was eight years old when she was removed. Carol was born in Broome in the mid-1950s and when she was three, her mother died leaving four children. Although her grandmother was still alive, Carol and her brothers and sisters were sent to the Beagle Bay dormitories where Carol spent the next fourteen years.

This is a story of generations of one family being disrupted. Like a terrible litany Carol can recall the exact timetable that was followed at the Beagle Bay Mission. The girls went barefoot except for high religious occasions when, Carol says, 'It felt real good to wear shoes and nice dresses for only an hour or so'. It is a story of repeated psychological and sexual abuse, dispossession and denial.

FIVE GENERATIONS OF MY family have been affected by removal of children. Four generations of my family have been removed from their mothers and institutionalised. Three generations of my family have been put into Beagle Bay Mission dormitories. Four generations of my family went without parently love, without mother or father. I myself found it very hard to show any love to my children because I wasn't given that, so was my mother and grandmother.

When I think back on my childhood days—sad, lonely and unloved childhood days—we should have been treated better than we were by the Church. We were mistreated badly, I was abused by the missionaries from all angles—sexual, physical and mental. I am a strong person in myself. I had to be strong, I had no-one to turn to, no-one to guide me through life.

6.30am every morning, straight from bed, we had to kneel and say our morning prayers. 7am we had to go to church for mass. If we didn't we would be punished, like going without a piece of bread for breakfast or get the strap or whipped on our palms. 7.30am we had to thank God before and after our breakfast. 10am we had to say another prayer before we had our cups of milk and morning tea break. 11am we had catechism taught to us which was part of praying and learning about the history of our church. 12pm again we said our prayers before and after our lunch. 1pm we said another prayer before and after class. 5pm we prayed again before and after our supper. 6pm most times we had to go to church for Benediction or rosary. 7pm we would kneel and say the last prayer of the day, which was our night prayers.

We were locked up every night. Also during the day on weekends and public holidays. That was only when we didn't go out on picnics.

7am breakfast—very light which was only sago with milk or most times porridge. 10am morning tea time: one cup of Carnation milk. 12am lunch, very light sometimes one piece of bread covered with lard along with a small piece of boiled meat. We loved it all the same.

5pm supper, very light which was 'bubble-bubbles' which was only flour, sugar and water, and if we were lucky we would have a piece of fruit.

We had nothing else to eat, only if we stole vegetables from the garden. We had two big vegetable gardens. Every vegetable was grown there yet we were never given any. We never had vegetables. Things that we never saw on our meal table yet were sold elsewhere from Beagle Bay Mission. When it was my turn to work in the convent kitchen I saw that all the vegetables that our people grew were on their meal tables.

Everyone would think we were doing the laundries for a big hospital, how many times and how we washed the missionaries' laundry. Every Sunday evening we had to soak the missionaries' laundry. Every Monday morning we washed clothes by hands or scrubbing board. We then had to rinse and put into the big boilers. Then rinsed, then starched, then rinsed, then squeezed and hung out to dry. We had to iron all the clothes, plus mending and darning.

We made our clothes for the girls and the boys that were in the dormitory. We never was given footwear, only when and if we were making our first communion, confirmation or crowning of Our Lady. It felt real good to wear shoes and nice dresses for only an hour or so.

We were treated like animals when it came to lollies. We had to dive in the dirt when lollies were thrown to us. The lollies went straight into our mouths from the dirt. We had to, if it was birthday or feast day of the missionaries, wish them a happy day, take our lollies and run, knowing what could happen. We had to sometimes kiss the missionaries on the lips, or touch their penises. I remember clearly on one occasion, I was told to put my hands down his pants to get my lolly.

The nuns taught us that our private parts were forbidden to touch. If we were caught washing our private parts, we would get into trouble from the nuns. I grew up knowing that our private parts were evil, yet missionaries could touch us when they felt like it. That is why when I grew up that I automatically thought when a man wanted sex that I had to give it to him, because that's what, y'know. Sometimes I had sex not for pleasure, but just to please the man.

Even at the dormitory, when we used to complain to the nuns about what the brothers and the priests had done to us, we were told to shut our mouths. That's why they used to always tell me I'm a troublemaker. Those same priests, they're still alive, they're still working down south. Even the nuns are still here in Broome; there's a couple of them still there.

It never happened to me, but I remember the priest...used to just walk into the dormitory and pick any girl out of the crowd, 'You, come with me', and take them. And I noticed, when those girls used to come back they were very upset. I can't say what really happened there, but 'til this very day, those people don't go to church.

The thing that hurt me the most while growing up is that we were pulled away from our sisters and brothers. My sister's a year younger than I, yet I could not hold her, cry with her, play with her, sleep with her, comfort her when someone hit her, and eat with her. We weren't allowed to be close to our sisters or brothers. The missionaries pulled and kept us apart.

I was taken out of school when I was only 15 years of age by the nuns and placed with the working girls. I had no further education. To leave the mission I had to have two people to sort of say they'd look after me. [Carol lived with an aunt and worked as a domestic for a family in Broome.] I remember being reminded many times about being sent back to Beagle Bay if I did not do my work properly or not listening to them. I did not want to go back there, so I had no choice but to listen. This is one of many times I felt trapped. I was treated like a slave, always being ordered to do this or do that, serving visitors and being polite to them.

[At 19, Carol gave birth to a son.] I had no-one to guide me through life, no-one to tell me how to be a good mother. A year later I fell pregnant with my second child. My son was only a year old and I kept being reminded by the Welfare and by my so-called family that they'd take my babies away from me. So instead of giving them the pleasure of taking my baby, I gave her up. I was still working for the M family and I was encouraged by a few people. My daughter was removed from my arms by policy of Welfare 5 days after she was born. I never saw my daughter for 20 years, until 2 years ago. He [Carol's employer] more or less encouraged me to put my baby up for adoption. Two months after that, he got me in bed. We had a relationship for so long— 4 or 5 years. And then I had a daughter to him. And this is what my trouble is now. I found my daughter, the one I gave up for adoption; but the last one, Tina, she's about 18 now, Mr M never gave me one cent for my daughter for the last 16 years. About a year ago he started helping me out, but then his wife found out, so now he won't help me. So my daughter now has to live in the same town as Mr M, knowing her father's in the same town, yet we could go without food. I reckon he should recognise her, stand up to his responsibilities.

The following anecdotes did not appear in the Report. They give a vivid picture of Carol's impression of her life.

CHICKEN FARM

We would have one of the largest Chicken Farms. We had to steal just to have a taste. I remember I, along with a few other girls, were so hungry that we decided to steal some vegetables, each of us killed a chicken, each threw it in the fire with the feathers and guts still attached. We pierced holes on both ends of the eggs. When we had enough, we took the rest back for our young sisters, then we got caught sneaking back into the dormitory. We were punished.

COOL DRINK FACTORY

We had a big cool drink factory. When, and if we were given a cool drink, one bottle was shared between six girls. We were also given cool drinks on special occasions. I was sometimes lucky because my uncle used to work there.

VEGETABLES

We had two big vegetable gardens. Every vegetable you can name was grown there and yet we were not given any at meal times. My brother worked at the gardens.

GOAT FARM

I remember tasting a lot of goat's milk, but never eating goat's meat. I was a bit lucky because my Grandmother was in charge of the other girls who were milking the goats. I was allowed to go along with her.

BUTCHER SHOP

We had a lot of wild cattle around which was killed, then cut up at the Butcher shop. We hardly ate beef, if we did it was just boiled up.

BAKER SHOP

We ate a lot of bread. That was one thing we had a lot of, maybe because flour was so cheap. I've never tasted bread as good as what my uncle baked at Beagle Bay.

WEEDING AND GARDENING

We had a lot of experience with spades, shovels, hoes, rakes, again we ended up with blistered hands, we had to work the whole of the mission. We had to pick up Horse and Bullock manure, put them in a forty-four drum of water, after being soaked for a month, we had to pour it on the plants and trees, and it stank.

SEWING AND MENDING

We had about five sewing machines in the sewing room. We made our own clothes for the boys and girls that were boarding in the dormitories. We were also taught how to do a proper patch on torn clothing.

POLISHING AND WAXING

We had to polish all copper and silver ware until they shone. We also polished the wooden verandas on our hands and knees, then went over the floors with the big polishers, we had to do it properly until we could see our faces in it.

COOKING FOR THE MISSIONARIES

Cooking for the Missionaries was the best job on the mission. When it was my turn to work in the Convent kitchen, I then saw that all the vegetables that our people grew were on their meal tables, that also was the first time that I have seen a decent meal served to any human being and it looked delicious. We were also taught how to cook a good meal for the whites, we were taught how to dish and lay it out in style, also how to set the tables.

FIRST-BORN

I found that when I gave birth to my eldest and first-born, I found that my son was the first thing that

I could give and receive love from.

I could call my own,

I didn't have to share him with anyone else,

My son if the first person, who was ever close to me.

I am also certain that my Grandmother and my Mother would have made the same above statement as I have just made. Our first-borns are very important to us all.

While growing up at Beagle Bay we had to share everything with the other children, including our underwear. We had nothing that we could call our own. The only thing we owned was ourselves. I do feel very hurt for people who were removed and also had their first-born child taken away from them.

NATIVE NUNS

A large group of our young women joined the nunnery. I don't know much about the native Sisters. But I do know that my mother joined because she wanted to eat jelly and custard. When she had enough of the good food, she took her nun's clothes off and put her ordinary clothes on and joined the other girls.

That story was told to me by a nun, that is the first and only time anyone has ever told me a full story about my mother. That is also the first time that I actually cried my heart out. I have heard bits and pieces of stories about my mother.

The same nun gave me a photo of my mother. I got four copies which I gave to my brother and sister. My sister wouldn't take it stating, 'How do we know this is our mother?' I was stuck for words. My sister was right. I should have comforted and cried with her, but I didn't. I didn't know how because it was never done to me so we both had a cry away from each other.

MY MOTHER

People always commented on how beautiful she was, kind, very outgoing, bubbly personality and so natural. I am so much like my mother, everything she was, I am. The only difference is that my mouth is bigger, plus our people didn't have the power to speak up for their rights so I honestly believe that our generation has more opportunities and power, and I am going to make sure that the world knows what really happened to our people.

[Carol has tried to document her stay at Beagle Bay but has been told there is no record she was ever there.] I haven't got anything to say I've been to Beagle Bay. It's only memories and people that I was there with. I don't exist in this world. I haven't got anything, nothing to say who I am.

11

Tony's Story

IN THIS STORY OF a life which seems to have been almost completely shattered, the focus is on the colour of Tony's skin. Because he is so dark he is seen by his foster mother as 'a disappointment'. He is constantly being robbed of affection and care, and the lack of love in his life can be seen to be directly related to the crimes he has committed. The story also contains a remarkable and tragic twist of fate. Confidential submission number 82.

IN 1967 I WAS adopted into a white family. They had two sons of their own. It is documented that, from an early age, my adoption mother had feelings of rejection towards me. She wanted a white son. She was taking offence to me as I grew up and my skin got darker. I can remember her always making fun of me. She had a favourite song that she always sung to me. It was that old country song called, 'The biggest disappointment in the family is you'. They adopted another son and my new brother was very fair, with blue eyes and blond hair.

As I grew up, more problems arose. I began to notice that I was getting darker. My adoption father was often sticking up for me when my adoption brothers would come home and tease me about my colour. They were learning words like, boong, coon, abo…I'd ask her why I was dark. She would tell me it was because I kept playing with aboriginal kids at school. My adoption mother would make me feel guilty when I got into trouble for something. She would confirm her statement by saying things like, '…if you keep playing with aborigines, you'll end up turning into one'. I was beginning to believe that was why I was getting darker. I started to hate what I was turning into. I started to hate my own people.

In 1978 I went to high school. I was to be separated again. This time it was from my adoption brothers. They were sent to one high school and I was sent to another. When I wanted to know why, my adoption mother told me that she didn't want me to embarrass her sons.

Towards the end of 1978, I was running away from home and truanting from school. I was sick of my adoption family. I hated my adoption mother. I wanted them to send me back to the orphanage. I wanted my real mother. I didn't belong where I was. I just wanted to go back to where I believed my mother would come and get me one day. I committed my first offence at eleven. I was trying to make my adoption family hate me so they'd send me back. I ended up back at the orphanage. When the welfare officer questioned me about my behaviour, I told him that I wanted to have my real family. He kept telling me that it was impossible. I didn't believe him and persisted in asking for many years to follow.

After a few months at the orphanage I was getting blamed for things that I wasn't doing. On one occasion I was blamed for starting a fire in the building. I never did it. They wanted to foster me with white families. I ran away. I was sick of getting into trouble and I was scared about being fostered. I just wanted my real family. I couldn't understand why they wouldn't take me home.

[After some months on the streets in Brisbane, at the age of thirteen Tony was taken into care as uncontrollable.]

While at Wilson [youth centre] I felt like I was in a prison. In my mind, I hadn't done anything wrong to be sent there. I spent months asking what I'd done wrong. They told me that I was uncontrollable. I used to cry a lot. I kept asking the social workers to find my real mother. It was the same old story.

I ran away a few times. When I escaped I used to go to a family I'd met. They had aboriginal foster kids. I used to like going there. I felt that I had something in common with these kids. Everyone there liked me. The parents there treated me as if I was one of their own kids. I ended up getting caught and sent back to Wilson. I was depressed again. The family who I'd stayed with made several attempts at fostering me. The welfare department blocked all attempts. I didn't know how to feel. All this time, the welfare couldn't wait to put me into a home. Then when I found a family that I wanted to stay with on my own, they wouldn't allow it. It was like nobody cared what I wanted. It was as if I had no say in anything. It was being arranged for me to be adopted again by another family. When I became aware of this, I did what I was beginning to do best, run away. This made matters worse. People were beginning to give up on me. I was finally sent to Boys Town [aged nearly fourteen].

I ran away from Boys Town several times. On one occasion that I ran away, I caught a train back up to Townsville. One of the passengers—a woman travelling with her boyfriend—took care of me. We got on real good. She had brown skin just like me. This woman kept asking me questions about who I was and where I came from. I was a runaway, so I was restricted to how much I could say, in fear of being caught. I was in love with this woman. I remember falling asleep with my head on her lap. We talked each other to sleep.

The following day we arrived at Townsville station. She asked me if I had anywhere to stay. I told her no. Her and her boyfriend invited me to stay with them. I stayed only two days with them. She washed my clothes and made sure that I had a good feed. On the second day she went out with her boyfriend. I got jealous of her boyfriend and ran away when they left.

Until the age of twenty-eight I wasn't aware just how close I was to finding my mother.

Later the next day I was arrested by the Townsville police. [Tony was returned to Boys Town where he stayed until he turned fifteen. He then found employment.]

It was a difficult time in my life. It was then that I was mature enough to realise the full ramifications of what everything was building up to. I started to convince myself that I was destined to spend the rest of my life alone. I often saw old people in the street, who were obviously homeless, and knew that that was how I was going to end up. I used to get really depressed about that. Those thoughts and feelings stayed with me for a very long time.

I was never sent back to my family. [When Tony was aged seventeen his welfare officer recommended reintroduction to his birth family. The recommendation was ignored.] Nobody cared about the pain that I was feeling. So I tried my best to hide from it. Antisocial behaviour seemed the only way that I could deal with my problems for years to follow. I've been a loner since then.

[At sixteen Tony stole a car from the family with whom he was staying and left the State. At eighteen he committed a burglary and spent ten months in prison.]

When I got out I started making contact with my adoption family by phone. It was becoming positive. My adoption mother refused me permission to go home to them when I got my holidays from work. She claimed that, '…dad doesn't think it's a good idea'. That hurt me a lot. A year later I tried to contact them again. This time my adoption father answered the phone. I rang up to wish my adoption mother a happy birthday. When I asked, '…is mum there?', I was told that she had died two months earlier. It devastated me. While I was on the phone, I made it clear to my adoption father that I loved him. I felt terrible because I never got to say it to my adoption mother. I'd spent the previous two years trying to make amends.

My life fell apart once again. I became a drug addict and started to abuse alcohol and everyone around me.

Tony was soon convicted of robbery with wounding in company. He is serving a fourteen-year sentence. Link-Up, in Queensland, located his family in 1993. His mother had died nine years earlier. She had been the woman on the train.

12

Karen's Story

KAREN'S LIFE HAS TAKEN her away, not only from her family but also from her country. She lives in New Zealand and says that she has a sense of not really belonging anywhere. This is Confidential submission number 823 New Zealand.

I AM A PART Aboriginal woman, who was adopted out at birth. I was adopted by a white Australian family and came to live in New Zealand at the age of six months. I grew up not knowing about my natural Mother and Father. The only information my adoptive parents had about my birth, was the surname of my birth Mother.

I guess I had quite a good relationship with my adoptive Mum, Dad and sisters. Though my adopted Mother said I kept to myself a lot, while I was growing up. As I got older I noticed my skin colouring was different to that of my family. My Mother told me I was adopted from Australia and part Aboriginal. I felt quite lonely especially as I approached my teens. I got teased often about being Aboriginal and became very withdrawn and mixed up, I really did not know where I belonged.

As a result of this I started having psychiatric problems. I seemed to cope and muddle along.

I eventually got married to a New Zealander, we have two boys, who are now teenagers. One of our boys is dark like myself, and was interested in his heritage. I was unable to tell him anything, as I didn't know about it myself.

My husband, boys and myself had the opportunity to go to Melbourne about seven years ago on a working holiday for ten weeks. While in Melbourne I went to the Aboriginal Health Centre and spoke to a social worker, as I had a copy of my birth certificate with my birth Mother's name on it. The social worker recognised my Mother's surname, Graham, and got in touch with my aunty, who gave me my Mother's phone number.

I got in touch with my birth Mother and made arrangements to meet her. I have a half-brother and sister. My birth Mother and Father never married, though my Father knew my Mother was pregnant with me. My Mother did not know where my Father was, as they parted before I was born. My sister decided to call a local Melbourne paper and put our story in the paper on how I had found them after twenty-nine years.

My Father, who was in Melbourne at the time, saw the article and a photo of my Mother and myself in the paper. He recognised my Mother and got in touch with her. My Mother and I had been corresponding, after we returned to New Zealand.

For her own reasons, she would not give my Father my address, so my Father went through the social service agency and got in touch with me two and half years ago. I have met my birth Father, as I had a family wedding in Melbourne shortly after he made contact with me, so I made arrangements to meet him.

We kept in contact with one another, but I feel we will never be able to make up for lost time, as my birth parents live in Australia and myself in New Zealand.

I still feel confused about where I belong, it has been very emotional and the result of this caused me to have a complete nervous breakdown. I am on medication daily and am having to see a counsellor to help me come to terms and accept the situation, where I am at right now and to sort out some confused feelings. My adoptive family really don't want to know too much about my birth family, which also makes it hard.

I feel that I should be entitled to some financial compensation for travel purposes, to enable us to do this.

13

Lance's Story

LANCE'S MOTHER LOVES HIM, but he hates her because she allowed him to be taken away from her. He says that if anyone tried to take his own children, it would be over his dead body. As a child he hated himself and wished that God would make him white. This is Confidential submission number 154.

DAD DIED WHEN I was about two. My parents were married, but they often lived apart. When I was a little kid, they gave me to an Uncle and Auntie and the police took me away from them and put me in a Home. I have never been with my brothers and sisters at all. They were also put into the same Home. My brothers and sisters did not know that I existed until a nun said, 'Come and meet your little brother'. I have some contact with them now. I see them once every six months. To me they are like acquaintances.

If I was in a stable Aboriginal family, I wouldn't have the problems I have now—identifying myself as Koori. For ages I despised my parents; how could they just dump me in this Home? I hated them for what they were—Koories. I therefore hated Koories. I hated myself because I was Koori.

St Joseph's Home, Sebastopol, is where I grew up. It was run by nuns wearing black habits. The only Aboriginal kids there were just me and another bloke. There were girls there too. I stayed there for seven or eight years. I bloody hated it. I remember going to bed crying every night and wetting the bed every night and every day moping around unhappy. I hated authorities. The nuns were really strict on you. We had a big dormitory where the boys slept. I used to go to bed crying. I remember a nun with a torch saying, 'Stop crying'. I hid my head. She came back and hit me on the head with the torch. I still have the scar today.

I did not know I had brothers and sisters until I was aged twelve. I thought, 'How come I did not know about it? Where were they? How come they did not come and play with me?' You did not really want to know them and find out Mum and Dad kept them and threw you away. You'd realise your fears were true.

Lake Condah Mission is where my parents came from. I suspect they grew up with their parents. My parents moved around heaps, although my mother doesn't now. We have a love–hate relationship. She loves me, but I hate her. I have never had a Birthday Card or Christmas Card. She is just a Mum in that she gave birth to me.

At age eight I was adopted out to these white people. They had three children who were a lot older—in their thirties and forties. I get on with them well. They send me Christmas Cards and Birthday Cards. It is good having people like that, but sometimes you know you are not really part of the family. You feel you should not really be there, for example: 'Come along Lance, we're having a family photo taken'. I have not told them how I feel. They have tried real hard to make me feel part of the family, but it just won't work.

I got up to Year Eleven at school. I got a lot of flak, 'How come your parents are white?' On Father and Son Day, 'Is he the Postman or what?' It was pretty awkward. It was always awkward. I was always a shy kid, especially among my Father's friends. 'Here is my son.' They would look at you. That look.

'You're still together?' I remember waiting for my Mother at her work, which was a bakery. A bloke asked me, 'Where is your Mum?' He searched for an Aboriginal lady. I wished God would make me white and these people's son instead of an adopted son.

I still call them Mum and Dad. But when I go to my real Mum, I find it real hard to call her my 'Mum' because she has just been another lady, OK a special lady. Mum's Mum [that is, adoptive mother] because she was there when I took my first push-bike ride and went on my first date.

After Year Eleven, I got a couple of jobs. I got into heaps of trouble with the Police—drugs and alcohol. I could get my hands on it and escape and release my frustration. I saw Police...their fault as well as with me being taken away from my family. Slowly that decreased because a couple of cops came to my place, just to see how I was doing and just to talk to me. You can see the effects of stuff, such as alcohol, so I don't drink anyway. Alcohol took me away from my parents, who are chronic alcoholics. Mum is and Dad was. It took my brother [car accident at eighteen years, high blood alcohol reading].

Three years ago I started taking interest in Koori stuff. I decided at least to learn the culture. I did not find the stereotype. I found that we understood what we were and that we were on a wave length. I made a lot of friends and I am yet to make more. It becomes very frustrating. I am asked about a Koori word and I don't know. You feel you should know and are ashamed for yourself. I feel Koori, but not a real Koori in the ways of my people.

It is hard to say whether I was better off being taken away because the alternative never happened I think the people I went with were better off economically and my education was probably better than what it would have been otherwise. I might have ended up in jail. I may not have had two meals or none and fewer nice clothes and been less well behaved.

If someone tried to remove my kids—over my dead body. I'd pack them up and move them away. Not the shit I've been through—no.

14

Peggy's Story

PEGGY SPEAKS OF BEING 'birthed out in the trees', 'under the stars' and goes on to tell how her family became 'caught up in the system' and scattered.

Although Peggy was kept with her mother in a dormitory for Indigenous women, when she was four, she and her mother were separated and could only see each other through a chicken-wire fence. The story of Peggy's life in the dormitory is drawn in vivid detail. This is Confidential evidence number 404.

MY FAMILY WENT TO Cherbourg. They volunteered to go there during the Depression. So I would have been about six months old when grandfather, who was, I mean, he was independent. He had eight kids all birthed out in the trees you know, under the stars. My mother spoke her own language. She had me with the promise to marry my father. And then when the Depression came they talked to the policeman. He said go to Buramba. When things get better come back out again. He was the Protector so he sent them there. The thing is though, when we got there you got caught up in the system. You weren't allowed out any more.

The decision that my grandfather made at the time, he didn't know that that would split his whole family up.

My Dad was away. He thought we had died. He didn't know what had happened. No-one else seemed to know where we had disappeared to. The whole family went to Cherbourg. Mum said when they got there they were immediately split up. Mum said the superintendent said, 'Agnes, you can't live in the camp with your small baby and you have to go into the dormitory'.

Mum thinks that's just…She won't talk about it. She's in denial. She said they did it for our good because there was no room in the camp. But I said, 'You lived in Ayumba with your old people when you was outside. Why would it now be different that you didn't want to live with them?'

She said, 'Well, they offered the dormitory to me, so I took you there'. I was six months old. Because the dormitory is such a big place and it's made up, you know…it's split that way [in half] downstairs with your women that side, your girls that side.

I stayed with my Mum for four years on that side with the other mothers. The boys went into the boys' home—my grandfather's sons. And he had Mum's younger sister and younger brother—they stayed with the old people. But the rest of them—the boys—were put in a home. Mum was put in the dormitory.

I stayed with her until I was four years of age. You slept with your mother because there was basically no room for a cot or anything and for four years you're there living with her.

But when I turned four, and because I was such an intelligent child, sneaking off to school because all the other kids are going… matron made the decision that, 'Peggy has to go to school'. And so immediately that decision was made, I was transferred over to this section. I was taken from her. Separating her from me was a grill. There was chicken-wire across there. That was the extent of how far you could go to this [other] side.

Once you were separated from your Mum, you're not to go back to her again. Absolutely no interaction. You have a bed on your own. No contact during the day. I'm out of her control. She is no longer actually my mother, type of thing. So you go under the care and control of the Government. That's what happened.

No-one said anything to me. No-one said anything to her, but everybody else in that section knew that this is what happened. And most of those women, my mother tells me, kept their children on the breast for a long, long time, because that bonding was going to be broken at some stage and so keeping their children close to them was the only thing that they had. I've always been an angry child. Very angry. I don't remember much about this section with my mother. I remember nothing. It embarrasses me when she talks of me running to her for cuddles and she'll say, 'I fed you on my titties'. And I get rather embarrassed because I don't remember that time with her.

But I can remember sitting here at this grill on that side waiting for her to come out of the door of one of these wards here so that I can just see her. She wouldn't come out because it hurt her to see me over this side. I turned five around about July. I went to school, but then she had to go to work. So we had that removal from our grandparents, her family, then I was removed from her and I then became the victim.

She ate on this side and I ate on that side. Birthdays were arranged. No, I never saw her on birthdays. I got a cake every birthday that was arranged by the Government—only because she fought for it.

I didn't get to know her. To me she was just the woman who comes and goes. When I was five she went again. They sent her out to work. I remember the night the taxi pulled up to take her.

Again, there was nothing emotional because if you were a little girl on this side you got into trouble for crying. You couldn't show emotion. Here at this wire grill I could just hear the director of the management call out to me, 'Is that you, Peggy?' They could just see my little form there sitting at the wire grill.

'You don't get to bed, you'll be punished!' And so, go to bed. If I'm crying at night, 'Is that you, Peggy, crying again?' And so it just went on. You've got about sixty or seventy other kids there, so why cry for your mother because kids are going to look after you and think 'she's crying for her mother'? You got to show your anger some place.

I remember that night. We had to sing prayers at night, and I could catch up, I mean, it didn't take me long to know what the system is all about. You're better off living within that system rather than out of it. You go with it. I remember singing prayers that night:

> Now the day is over
> Night is drawing near

This always upsets me because at the end of singing that prayer, I couldn't remember the words. 'Cause I've got a very high voice—a lot higher than a lot of the kids—they'd hear me first.

> Meadows of the evening
> Creep across the sky
> La la la la la la la la

> Getting higher and higher

> Four and twenty blackbirds
> Baked in a pie.

That ended the prayer and the old lady called out, 'Is that you, Peggy? Get out here'. And I had to kneel on the floor till everyone went to sleep.

It was all about control, reform. The bald head was part of the dormitory system for punishment. If you had lice, you had your head shaved. But you could have your hair cut off for being naughty, doing anything naughty. it didn't matter what it was:

speaking back, not doing your chores. Cold baths, getting your hair shaved off if you didn't go for wood in the afternoon so you could warm the baths up.

You also got the strap and you got put into jail. There was three components of the punishment that you got. You could even be left without any food. Go without your meal. Stand in the middle of the dining room there while everybody else finished. Many times I stood there. Humiliation, because when you got your head shaved we were not allowed to put a beret or anything on our heads. Not allowed.

So you walked to school like this and the camp kids made fun of you and that would bring us closer together as a group. As a group [dormitory kids] we were able to fight off the other kids and their insults to us.

We were called the dormitory girls. But the kids who slept out on the verandah—they break my heart and it still upsets me: they were the 'pee-the-beds'. They were called nothing else but pee-the-beds. Maybe you'd pee the bed one night because you were upset tummy, fear, no electric light just a flickering light of an old hurricane lamp. It would scare you because old people have the habit of telling you there's people walking around here at night time. All these 'woop-woops' around the place. And you didn't want to go to the toilet and you may wet the bed. It may only be a one night occurrence, but you transferred from your bed out onto the verandah. You slept on a mattress on the floor and all you were called was pee-the-beds. 'Tell the pee-the-beds they've gotta get their mattresses in off the line.' 'Tell the pee-the-beds they've gotta put their blankets out.' 'Tell the pee-the-beds it's time to get up.' No identity at all. Absolutely nothing. These kids were just grouped together.

I was talking to a young girl the other day. I said, 'Your mother never peed the bed but her sister did. She had to go down there to sleep with her sister because the kid was crying. She needed her sister with her.'

I could see them on a morning, a winter's morning. No ceiling. Just when the sun hit the tin roof. 'All you pee-the-beds gotta get up!' And they would get up out of their wet clothing and all you see is steam coming off them. It was absolutely dreadful and I grieve for those kids, honestly. We were cruelly treated.

15

William's Story

WHEN WILLIAM WAS A small boy sleeping in the caravan at his foster home, an unknown person came in and raped him. It happened often. He was moved from place to place, and he cried every night for his mother. Nobody told him his mother had died. This is Confidential evidence number 533.

I CAN REMEMBER THIS utility [truck] with a coffin on top with flowers. As a little boy I saw it get driven away knowing there was something inside that coffin that belonged to me. I think I was about six years old at the time. This was the time of our separation, after our mother passed away. My family tried to get the Welfare to keep us here...trying to keep us together. Aunty D in Darwin—they wouldn't allow her to keep us. My uncle wanted to keep me and he tried every way possible, apparently, to keep me. He was going to try and adopt me but they wouldn't allow it. They sent us away.

As a little kid I can't remember what was going on really, because I was a child and I thought I was going on a trip with the other brothers. I just had excitement for going on a trip. That's all I can think of at the time.

When St Francis [orphanage] closed up, they sent us out to

different places. My second eldest brother and I went to a Mrs R. And my only recollections of that lady was when we first went there. We were greeted at the door. The welfare officer took us into this house and I can remember going into this room, and I'd never seen a room like it. It was big, and here me and my brother were going to share it. We put our bags down on the floor. We thought, This is wonderful. As soon as the welfare officer left, Mrs R took us outside that room and put us in a two-bed caravan out the back.

I was sleeping in the caravan. I was only a little boy then. In the middle of the night somebody come to the caravan and raped me. That person raped me and raped me. I could feel the pain going through me. I cried and cried and they stuffed my head in the pillow. And I had nobody to talk to. It wasn't the only night it happened.

Oh God, it seemed like night after night. It seemed like nobody cared. I don't know how long it went on for, but night after night I'd see the bogey man. I never saw the person. I don't know who that person was.

Then we were all taken away again to a new home, to another place. We were shunted from place to place, still trying to catch up with schooling, trying to find friends. I had no-one. I just couldn't find anybody. And when I did have a friend I was shunted off somewhere else, to some other place. Wanting my mother, crying for my mother every night, day after day, knowing that she'd never come home or come and get me. Nobody told me my mother died. Nobody...

They shifted us again and that was into town again. And then they put us in with this bloke...They've got records of what he did to me. That man abused me. He made us do dirty things that we never wanted to do. Where was the counselling? Where was the help I needed? They knew about it. The guy went to court. He went to court but they did nothing for me, nothing. They sent us off to the Child Psychology Unit. I remember the child psychologist saying, 'He's an Aboriginal kid, he'll never improve. He's got behavioural problems'. I mean, why did I have behavioural problems? Why didn't they do anything?

I hit the streets of Adelaide. I drank myself stupid. I drank to take the pain, the misery out of my life. I couldn't stop. I smoked dope, got drugs. I tried everything. I did everything. I just couldn't cope with life. I lived under cardboard boxes. I used to eat out of rubbish bins. I'm so ashamed of what I've done.

I suffer today. I still suffer. I can't go to sleep at night. It's been on for years. I just feel that pain. Oh God, I wake up in the middle of the night, same time. My kids have asked me why I get up in the middle of the night and I can't explain it, I can't tell them—shamed. I can't sleep too well with it. I can't go to bed. I leave it till twelve o'clock sometimes before I go to bed. I lay there awake, knowing I'm gonna wake up at that time of the morning, night after night. I often wish I was dead. I often wish I was gone. But I can't because of my children. You can't explain this to your kids. Why did this happen? I had nobody.

I've had my secret all my life. I tried to tell but I couldn't. I can't even talk to my own brothers. I can't even talk to my sister. I fear people. I fear 'em all the time. I don't go out. I stay home. It's rarely I've got friends. I wish I was blacker. I wish I had language. I wish I had my culture. I wish my family would accept me as I am. We can't get together as a family. It's never worked. We fight, we carry on. I've always wanted a family.

16
Anne's Story

THIS STORY IS DIFFERENT in tone from the others collected here. Anne spent much of her early life in homes for Indigenous children, and also had the experience of being fostered to a white family where she was treated as a servant. Her narrative is part of a longer work that she is writing, and it is composed as autobiographical fiction. Her mother lets her be taken from the family in the hope that she will enjoy a better life, will learn to read and write. Anne did not in fact learn to read and write until she was an adult. She determined to educate herself and did so, ultimately going to university. Between the frightened child hoping for a better life and the woman who is now writing the story, is a lifetime of courage and determination. The optimism found in the mother in this story is still present in the daughter today. She speaks without bitterness and expresses always the hope that Australia will be able to move on, and that racial differences will be reconciled.

THE ABORIGINES DID NOT disappear, they lived out there, somewhere, out of sight and out of mind, and to be forgotten, in the pages of the history books. There were a few Aboriginal children who did escape through the net, only to be trained to feel and think as if they were white, while living in the shadows of their Aboriginality ashamed of their black skin colour.

I was one of those children, chosen to be fostered by a white family.

Mum kept on telling me how lucky I was to have such a wonderful opportunity in life, and a good education. Then she would smile at me and make me feel good inside, proud I was going to have an education. While telling me at the same time, 'Anne, I want you to be a good girl for these nice kind white people who live in Sydney. Otherwise they might think I have not brought you up properly. And don't forget to say your prayers at night'.

She told me that I would learn to read and write, and that I must write to her as often as I could because they would all be worried about me and would want to know if I was alright. She would get the mission manager, Mr N, to read the letters to her as soon as they arrived, because my mother could not read or write. Nobody in the family could. It was a government rule that Mr N would read my letters first even before my mother got them. All mail sent to the Aborigines first must be read by the mission manager, always.

'Anne, don't forget to write to your brother and sisters because they will be very proud of you, living with a rich white family in Sydney and getting an education. I can just see us now, showing all your letters to the other mission people and telling them about you and your new family who are giving you an education. They will be mighty proud of you and they will share a little bit of your joy. You know, Anne, I want you to go to Sydney with the Welfare Officer because you are my youngest child, and I think it would be wrong for me not to let you have this wonderful chance in life.'

Even at twelve years old I thought to myself, But Mum, don't you know, I love you and I don't want to leave you and the others. The only chance I ever want in life is to stay with you and my brother and sisters on the mission where I am happy.

One day Mr B arrived from the Aboriginal Welfare Board to take me to Sydney. Mum let me wear my old blue frock with a little white collar even though it was too short for me, she still let me wear it because she knew blue was my favourite colour.

Oh I love blue, the sky is blue,
the sea is blue,
even the brooch I found at the tip, for Mum, is blue,
Oh I love blue,
I feel so pretty standing here, near Mum, in my
pretty blue frock,
even with my black skin.

Not as though I had many frocks to choose from, and what few I did have were second hand, which were given by the people of the church to the mission for the Aborigines. I also wore a pair or old black shoes, without any socks, or shoe laces for that matter, and they too were given by the church.

We were poor, very poor, probably the poorest people in the country, but it didn't matter because I felt grand standing there beside Mum in my pretty blue frock, ready to go to Sydney. Even though in my heart I didn't want to go.

Soon we were surrounded by all the mission people with their children, standing there to say their goodbyes. Mum's sister Auntie Emma, and Uncle Peter were there too, with their three children. Trying to say their goodbyes were my two best friends Christine and Jennifer, while Mum was fussing over me, while talking at the same time. I can still hear Mum now, speaking softly.

'Be a good girl for the white people and don't forget your manners and don't forget to say your prayers. Before too long you will be able to read and write and send me your letters. Where is the handkerchief I gave you. Don't lose it, you might need it later. I have packed some Vegemite sandwiches for you and Mr B in case you get hungry.'

She continued talking, trying to say everything at once, while at the same time straightening the blue ribbon in my long black curly hair. Then Mum handed me a photo of the family, which was taken when I was a baby by old Billy Joe when he first came up to live at the mission. It made me feel sad, taking this photo from Mum, as it was the only one she had of all the family together.

I then looked up at Mum to see she was trying to hide the tears in her eyes, so I knew she was feeling bad inside. Suddenly she turned to my two sisters, Carol and Sarah, and my big brother Leslie, and she waved them over to come and say their goodbyes. Then she said to them, 'You might not see your baby sister Anne for a very long time. Now kiss her goodbye'.

A dreadful feeling of emptiness, like lightning striking me from inside, crippled me with fear. Then for the first time I realised the reality of the situation, I was leaving our dear loving Mother, my brother and sisters, my friends behind. I was leaving the only home I had ever known, the place where I was born only twelve years before. It took all my strength to hold back my tears so Mum wouldn't know how bad I felt inside.

Then Coral, who was two years older than me, gave me a lovely white pebble she found down by the creek, because she knew it would remind me of home. It would remind me of where we spent hours playing together in the water or just sitting near the water and talking to Mum. Or collecting tadpoles and stones. 'This pebble, Sis', she said, 'will remind you of the fun we had together'.

Then Coral kissed me goodbye and said she would miss me, and Mum would miss me because I was the youngest. Jennifer, who was a year older than me, pushed her way in, anxiously trying to give me a lovely pine cone which she had painted gold at the mission school.

After kissing me goodbye she went over to Mum. I think if she didn't she would've started to cry. Then my big brother Leslie, sixteen years old, gave me his special sensitive look which he always did whenever I was hurt, to let me know he cared. While Auntie Emma was comforting Mum, she kissed me goodbye, wiping the tears from her eyes and telling me to be a good girl for Mr B because he had come from Sydney specially to get me.

Then Mr B told me to pick up the few belongings I had and we left, with my family standing there among all the other mission people calling out their goodbyes. As we moved towards the mission gate I could still hear their voices in the distance, and if I turned round I could see them waving their handkerchiefs up into the sky.

With each step I took the distance grew further, and away, from Mum and the rest of the family. I began to wonder how long it would be before I would see my family again, or if I would ever see them again. The thought frightened me, so I walked with my head turned back, looking at them, before they disappeared, out of sight, out of my life. It was like my brain was taking a photograph of each of their faces, my eyes focused, imprinting them into my memory.

I was trying to keep up with Mr B, not sure of how much was real or what was my previous memories from the past. But it made me realise how lovely my family really were. I had taken them for granted and now I was leaving them behind, walking out of their lives off to who knows where.

I can see my mother's face now, growing sadder and sadder. My brother's large black eyes and high cheek bones which made him look so handsome. Coral and Emma with their olive skin and green eyes. They were so beautiful. I remembered Auntie Emma and Mum always having the same conversation every time Auntie Emma came over for a cup of tea.

Auntie Emma would say how handsome Leslie was and how pretty the girls were. And Mum would say that the high cheek bones and the green eyes were inherited from our father who was German. We had heard it all a thousand times before, and this was the only thing I ever heard about my father. For some reason we never asked Mum any questions about him.

I was thinking all these things as I was walking along with Mr B. Suddenly he interrupted me and said we must hurry or we would miss the train. Before long my family were completely out of sight. They were out of my life. Some of them I would never see again. And the others I would not see for many years to come. I looked up at the sky to hide my tears, just as it was beginning to rain.

17
Fiona's Story

WHEN FIONA, AGED FIVE, and her brothers and sisters were delivered to the mission at Oodnadatta, their mother 'just kind of disappeared into the darkness', and Fiona did not see her for another thirty-two years. Fiona says that maybe the most precious thing she lost while in the mission was her native language. She explains that the loss of this language is a loss of the soul.

However, she acknowledges the education she received from the missionaries, and doesn't like to hear harsh criticism of them. Her final comment is powerfully tragic and unintentionally ironic when she says: 'You have to learn to forgive'. This is Confidential submission number 305.

1936 IT WAS. I would have been five. We went visiting Ernabella the day the police came. Our great-uncle Sid was leasing Ernabella from the government at that time so we went there.

We had been playing all together, just a happy community and the air was filled with screams because the police came and mothers tried to hide their children and blacken their children's faces and tried to hide them in caves. We three, Essie, Brenda and me together with our three cousins...the six of us were put on the old truck and taken to Oodnadatta which was hundreds of miles away and then we got there in the darkness.

My mother had to come with us. She had already lost her eldest daughter down to the Children's Hospital because she had infantile paralysis, polio, and now there was the prospect of losing her three other children, all the children she had. I remember that she came in the truck with us curled up in the foetal position. Who can understand that, the trauma of knowing that you're going to lose all your children? We talk about it from the point of view of our trauma but—our mother—to understand what she went through, I don't think anyone can really understand that.

It was 1936 and we went to the United Aborigines Mission in Oodnadatta. We got there in the dark and then we didn't see our mother again. She just kind of disappeared into the darkness. I've since found out in the intervening years that there was a place they called the natives' camp and obviously my mother would have been whisked to the natives' camp. There was no time given to us to say goodbye to our mothers.

From there we had to learn to eat new food, have our heads shaved. So one day not long after we got there my cousin and I...we tried to run back to Ernabella. We came across the train. We'd never seen a train before and it frightened the hell out of us with the steam shooting out. So we ran back to the mission because that was the only place of safety that we knew. She was only four and I was only five.

Then we had to learn to sleep in a house. We'd only ever slept in our wilchas and always had the stars there and the embers of the fire and the closeness of the family. And all of a sudden we had high beds and that was very frightening. You just thought you were going to fall out and to be separated. There was a corridor and our cousins were in another room. We'd never been separated before. And the awful part was we had to get into that train later on with one little grey blanket and go down to Colebrook...a matter of weeks after. From that time until 1968 I didn't see [my mother]. Thirty-two years it was.

[I stayed at Colebrook] till 1946 [when] I was fourteen or fifteen. We were trained to go into people's homes and clean and look after other people's children. I went to a doctor and his wife. They were beautiful people. I stayed with them a couple of years. I guess the most traumatic thing for me is that, though I don't like missionaries being criticised—the only criticism that I have is that you forbade us to speak our own language and we had no communication with our family. We just seemed to be getting further and further away from our people, we went to Oodnadatta first, then to Quorn next, then when there was a drought there we went to Adelaide and went out to Eden Hills and that's where we stayed till we went out to work and did whatever we had to do.

I realised later how much I'd missed of my culture and how much I'd been devastated. Up until this point of time I can't communicate with my family, can't hold a conversation. I can't go to my uncle and ask him anything because we don't have the language...

You hear lots and lots of the criticisms of the missionaries but we only learnt from being brought up by missionaries. They took some of that grief away in teaching us another way to overcome the grief and the hurt and the pain and the suffering. So I'm very thankful from that point of view and I believe that nothing comes without a purpose. You knew that in those days there was no possibility of going back because cars were so few and far between and the train took forever to get anywhere so how could a five year old get back to the people.

I guess the government didn't mean it as something bad, but our mothers weren't treated as people having feelings. Naturally a mother's got a heart for her children and for them to be taken away, no-one can ever know the heartache. She was still grieving when I met her in 1968.

When me and my little family stood there—my husband and me and my two little children—and all my family was there, there wasn't a word we could say to each other. All the years that you wanted to ask this and ask that, there was no way we could ever regain that. It was like somebody came and stabbed me with a knife. I couldn't communicate with my family because I had no way of communicating with them any longer. Once that language was taken away, we lost a part of that very soul. It meant our culture was gone, our family was gone, everything that was dear to us was gone.

When I finally met [my mother] through an interpreter she said that because my name had been changed she had heard about the other children but she'd never heard about me. And every sun, every morning as the sun came up the whole family would wail. They did that for thirty-two years until they saw me again. Who can imagine what a mother went through?

But you have to learn to forgive.

18
Donna's Story

DONNA WRITES UNDER HER own name, Donna Meehan. Her recollections of how she and her brothers were taken from their mother are vivid with potent detail. They were first published in *Novacastrian Tales* (Elephant Press, 1997) under the title 'Joy Ride'.

The *Novacastrian Tales* Project was awarded an Australian Reconciliation Award by the Council for Aboriginal Reconciliation in 1997. Donna speaks with passion but with an absence of bitterness as she tells of the strangeness, and hearbreak of her experiences, and of the kindness of her adoptive family. This story is part of a longer project which is Donna's autobiography.

THE FIRST TRAIN RIDE I took is as clear in my mind as if it had happened yesterday.

Mum had all us kids dressed up, our hair brushed which was only done for special days, and we were constantly reminded to use our manners. Barry, Widdy, Robby, Sooty and myself were put in the back seat of a taxi while mum sat in the front seat with the driver. The lady taxi-driver had known all the kids at the camp since their birth. I thought it was strange that mum and the driver didn't speak as we made our way along the bumpy red track leading from camp towards town.

As I watched the red dust swirling from behind the vehicle, I remembered we were all dressed up and on our way to the station for my first ride on the big steam train. We had always heard the faint train whistle from camp, and a few times we saw the clouds of smoke from the train, but I had never seen one close up. I sat impatiently in the back seat clicking my new shiny black shoes together and admiring the new dress I was given for the day. All my brothers also wore their new shoes with white socks, a white shirt and a little black bow tie. We knew everyone had to get dressed up to go on the train and we felt important, like the little rich kids from in town who often had train rides during the holidays.

When we arrived at the station we were surprised to see so many other kids and women waiting on the platform. All the children were happy and running in between the legs of their mothers, playing tips to fill in time. It wouldn't be long before the huge powerful black train pulled into the station. We could see dirty grey smoke from the chimney pouring into the air half a mile away. It was a rare treat for us kids at camp to climb into one of the uncle's cars and be driven into town, so, when it was time to take our seat on the train, we climbed aboard jubilantly anticipating the joy ride.

It took a few minutes to decide who would have the window seat or sit near the aisle. Then we kept changing places as to who sat next to who. Mum hadn't taken her seat yet, so we all took turns inspecting the toilet which fascinated us. We knew it wouldn't be long before the train pulled out, so we took our seats again. But we lost Sooty and Robby. When an old white woman in a red hat sat next to me, I changed seats with Barry, as she terrified me. Suddenly, I felt scared, and asked: 'Where's Mum?' Barry kept telling us: 'Mum'll be getting on the train in a minute.' I kept asking: 'Where's Sooty, Robby and Mum?' Barry said: 'They must be in the next car.' There were still lots of black women standing on the platform hugging one another.

With a sudden jerk, squealing of brakes and a loud puff of the steam engine, the train shunted forward. Fear gripped my little heart. Barry and Widdy had bewildered looks on their faces, glancing at me and then at one another. I stared out the window as we slowly pulled out of the station. I was very confused. I saw the women standing on the platform watching us and wailing. Then I saw her. There was my mum in her only good blue dress standing next to my aunts and our old grandmother. Just standing there. Standing there with tears rolling down their cheeks too fast to even wipe away. Then Mum waved a white hanky and I pressed my face against the window pane as hard as I could, watching her. Watching until her blue dress faded into a tiny blue daub of colour. I looked back at the station for as long as I could until it was out of sight.

The atmosphere of celebration and anticipation that initially filled the cabin had vanished and there now echoed the distressed calls of fearful broken-hearted children. 'Why didn't mother and grandmother get on the train?' I cried over and over. The white woman in the red hat sat beside me with clasped hands, expressionless. Barry reassured me: 'Mum will catch the next train. I'll look after you.' But he was crying too.

I didn't understand what had happened, or why mum had changed her mind, or why she would let us go anywhere without our aunty or grandmother to look after us. We were on that train for a very long time. I had run out of tears to cry. The flat country from home that was covered with warm red dirt was now very hilly and layered with trees, and the camps which were situated alongside the train track became more frequent and visible. The white woman corrected Barry as she overheard him telling Widdy and me that they were the camps of the white man, and said: 'They are called towns, and we are going to the city.'

The motion of the noisy train became monotonous and the heat of the day invaded the cabin. It was a long time between the bigger towns now. We saw flash houses and colourful gardens but very few people on the streets. I couldn't see any dumps or orchards. Barry was telling Widdy: 'All the blackfellas must be away working,' as there weren't any to be seen in the towns or bush we passed. All we saw were white people. Now and then, we heard youngens on the train sobbing. After a while, bored by the countryside, I must have fallen asleep, despite the sting in my eyes from having cried so much that morning.

When I woke, we were still on the train. It was dark. I was cold. Barry and Widdy huddled together to keep warm. The white woman gave me a tea towel to keep warm as there was no blanket. The noise of the train tracks, rattle of bridges, crying children and mozzies biting got annoying. I sat there reliving the events of the day. I always managed to come up with more questions than when I began. All three of us took turns sitting next to the white woman. She scared me by her silence and unfriendly face, not at all like the friendly ones back at camp or even the happy strangers we saw at the circus the other day.

I was homesick. It had been the longest and most confusing day of my life. I felt alone in the dark. The tears stung my eyes and hurt more than the mozzies as I realised for the first time in my life there was no-one to sing me to sleep.

When I awoke the next time, it was daylight. It must have been the longest night in my life. Barry and Widdy were still asleep. I wished they would wake up. I had so many questions to ask. This wasn't the joy ride that I thought was going to be so much fun. Suddenly, I had this awful pain inside. I never felt it before. I felt like screaming and waking the boys. I burst into tears and sobbed so hard I did wake my two brothers. I sobbed and sobbed and lost my breath so I couldn't talk. After a few minutes, I calmed down enough to mumble: 'Where are we going?' Barry didn't know. He suggested we wait at the next station till mum's train pulled in. We were so hungry by this time. The white woman pulled out some sandwiches from her large old brown bag and shared them with us. We seemed to chew in time with the clicketty clack of the train tracks. I was bored with looking at the same faces of the few people I could see in the train. I was in the window seat and we weren't allowed to walk around except to go to the toilet.

There wasn't much colour inside the train as the walls and ceiling were a drab dark brown and the seats a lighter brown. I concentrated on the bright red and yellow pattern on my new dress. Of course, it wasn't brand new, as mum had gone into town the day before and came back with an armful of clothes for us kids. She said she got them from the Aboriginal Inland Mission. I could hear some children fighting over their seats. I seemed to notice every cough and every sigh. It was very hot and I was glad we could have the window open a little so I could feel the fresh breeze on my face. Sometimes I could even catch a scent of the bush from the trees we passed. Sometimes I sat between my brothers, but then it got too hot or uncomfortable and I would go back to my seat next to the white woman. She never spoke. Occasionally, she would pull a mirror from her brown bag and comb her hair or put on lipstick. She would read for a little while from a newspaper, then fold it up and put it back in her bag. I wondered what else she had inside that bag.

Some time later, Widdy and Barry were told they had to get off at the next station but I wasn't allowed to go with them. Barry was upset and told the white woman: 'Mum said I have to look after the other kids. I promised.' The woman ushered the boys out of the train, saying: 'I'll look after Donna. You'll see your brothers and sister very soon.' I remember being so sad and frightened and alone. I was so sad as I looked at my brothers while our train pulled out of the station. I didn't take any notice who was with them or how many people were on the platform. It seemed to happen so fast. It was just awful. It made no sense. My poor little heart must have been so frightened and confused, but what could a five-year-old do about it?

The white woman sat with me and talked every now and then, but I kept looking out the window. After some time, she pointed towards the passing countryside. I looked and there was the biggest dam I ever saw. The woman explained that what I was looking at were boats, as I didn't know what they were, not having seen them before. They looked pretty sitting there on top of the water. The sun skipped across the surface. It looked like someone was throwing hundreds of stars into the water. It made me happy seeing the stars dancing on top of the water. It was so beautiful. How I wished I could just get off the train and sit and watch the water and the boats for a long time, but I was stuck on the horrible train. I was told this was the Hawkesbury River. Then the shiny water was out of sight.

My little bottom was stiff from sitting for so long in a confined space. The train was travelling very slowly now as we meandered through hills and then alongside the river. There were lots of trees and the smell of the bush was strong. I could hear birds singing, but I couldn't see them because they were hiding. The size of the green hills impressed me. The ground back home was flat. I felt we were very high on a hill now. I could see the tops of trees heading down to the river. I couldn't see the ground at all. Mother Earth was covered with hundreds of trees.

I wouldn't want to go for a walk in that bush. I knew there would be too many snakes. But I liked all the different shades of green from all the different shapes of trees. To help pass the time, I took particular notice of the leaves. Some of them had yellow tips and others red. Small purple flowers were attached to a vine that grew freely around tree trunks and even acted as an umbrella for smaller trees. The bush smelt fresh and crisp, different to the old bush from home. Now and then, I could hear birds calling, and when I heard the frightened call of a young bird, I could identify with it. For the first time, I too felt like a trapped, helpless baby bird.

I was interrupted by the white woman who went to the toilet and returned with a wet tea towel to briskly wash my face and brush my hair. She combed her hair with another brush and then applied red lipstick and placed gloves on her hands and the red hat on her head.

As I looked out the window, I could see a big town coming into view with lots of big houses and lots of cars. There was a screeching of brakes and a hiss from the steam engine. In between the clouds of steam and coal smoke, I could see lots of people standing on the platform. Only one thing was wrong. All the people were white. There were no other dark-skinned people, or blackfellas, as my uncle called them.

After a lot of shunting, the train eventually came to a halt. The woman told me: 'It's time to get off.' She took my hand and I followed. There were so many people, and I was trying to see where Robby and Sooty were, but I was too short. I couldn't see anything except white legs and lots of suitcases. There was a lot of noise from people talking and laughing. There were men in black uniforms getting suitcases off the train, and other men loading boxes. One man had a whistle that he liked blowing. There was another man yelling, telling people where they could catch the next train. Everyone was busy.

By this time, there was a dark boy with me, but I didn't know who he was. It looked like he was a couple of years older than me. We were much too frightened to speak, so we just sat on a bench. We had been told to sit and wait. The woman with the red hat went to get us a drink. I searched around looking for a familiar face, but I was lost in the crowd. All the men and women were wearing hats and gloves like the people at the circus. All the women wore lipstick, so I knew they got that from the white Santa man.

Just when I felt like getting up and running away, the woman returned. There was a tall man of dark complexion and a short white woman walking beside her. The two smiling strangers bent towards me and said: 'Hello, Donna.' I was told: 'This is your new mummy and daddy. They have a lovely house and animals. Now you go with them and they'll give you something to eat.'

They took my hand and led me away through the station and down a paved street where lots of different coloured cars were parked in a row. I even saw a ute, but it wasn't the white Santa man's car. This one was green in colour. I kept looking around for my brothers, or at least one of them, as I didn't want to go anywhere without them. I was told to sit in the back seat of a yellowish, creamy-coloured car that was the same shape as the white Santa man's car. Just then, I saw another car following us. I told myself Barry and the other boys were in that one and we were all going to the same camp.

I sat in the back seat, not speaking. The new dark man and white woman were speaking another language. Even though I didn't understand a word, I could see they were very happy. The woman would regularly turn around and look at me with a bright smile. I didn't smile back, just lowered my head and kept my eyes fixed on the floor of the car. I was still very frightened, but I could see these people were more friendly than the woman on the train. These were friendly strangers.

The car trip took a little while, but not too long. When it stopped, I could see the new camp which had a big white wooden house, lots of chooks and even a sheep or two. The house stood at the end of a dirt track and was surrounded by bush. I could smell the bush, and it was friendly and inviting. I could hear lots of happy birds whistling and talking to one another, and the chooks made me laugh as I watched them fighting. I heard a train in the distance, and the closer it got to the house, the more nervous I became. I suppose I thought I would be put on it for another long trip. I was pleased to watch it pass us by. I was just starting to feel safe again when I heard another vehicle arriving. It turned into the yard where we stood watching the train. When the car came to a stop, two older people got out. I thought this must be the aunt and uncle of the people who lived at this camp.

I waited for my brothers to climb out of the car but the old people were by themselves. I was very disappointed. The two older people made a big fuss over me, talking to me, but I wasn't talking to strangers. They told me how pretty I was and how pretty my new dress was. They took photos of me standing between the man and woman in whose car I had travelled. We stood in front of the chook house for a photo.

This was the day I arrived in Newcastle. It was 22 April 1960. I was collected from Broadmeadow Railway Station and then driven to my new home at Whitebridge, a suburb south of Newcastle. In time, I learnt the names of my new foster parents who were Mr and Mrs Tim Popov. The older couple who welcomed me to Newcastle were their good friends Mr and Mrs Reedman from Adamstown. Mr Reedman was a preacher and mum was a singer, so wherever Mr Reedman preached, mum would sing. That is how we spent Sundays for years. They were special days for all of us.

My new mum and dad were very loving towards me. It took many weeks for me to get used to my new dad as he was a very tall, strong man and I was fearful of his size. I would hide behind the kitchen door every day when he returned from work. I wasn't familiar with men, as I had always been looked after by my mum or aunts around the camp. I only saw my uncles briefly, so women had a strong influence upon me. The men were left to influence the young boys. Where were my brothers and all the people from the camp? What had happened to them all?

I soon got familiar with the new white house that had rooms inside. I loved playing with the tap water. I had never seen water flowing out of a pipe before. I spent my days running around the little farm chasing chooks or sheep, as there wasn't a dog to play with. The first gift Mr and Mrs Reedman gave me was highly valued. It was my very own little red table and chairs set. Someone from one of the Churches gave me my first gollywog and another lady at another Church gave me my first brand new teddy bear. These were my constant companions. I named the gollywog Barry, and the teddy bear was called Widdy, after my two eldest brothers. That way, they were with me every day of my life. I talked to them and kissed them and this made me feel close to them. How I wished they could come and live at this new camp called home.

Voices

THROUGHOUT THE REPORT, AS the history and practice of removal are examined, there are short quotations from dozens of submissions from Indigenous people. Unlike the longer stories, which develop as narratives, these anecdotes and comments are sudden snapshots which illuminate the Report, throwing into relief the quotations from official records. The voices of Indigenous people, describing their memories and frustrations and sorrows, rise up through the other formal voices.

> 'We may go home, but we cannot relive our childhoods. We may reunite with our mothers, fathers, sisters, brothers, aunties, uncles, communities, but we cannot relive the twenty, thirty, forty years that we spent without their love and care, and they cannot undo the grief and mourning they felt when we were separated from them. We can go home to ourselves as Aboriginals, but this does not erase the attacks inflicted on our hearts, minds, bodies and souls, by caretakers who thought their mission was to eliminate us as Aboriginals.'
>
> From Link-Up(NSW) submission number 186.

Since one of the aims of the early policies was to suppress Indigenous speech, many submissions make reference to the loss of original language. With the suppression of language went the erosion of culture, and consequently the loss of personal and tribal identity. Services which support Indigenous people have also submitted comments on the central importance of language.

> 'I wish I was blacker. I wish I had language. I wish I had my culture.'
> This is a quotation from William's Story, Confidential evidence number 553.

> 'My mother and brother could speak our language and my father could speak his. I can't speak my language. Aboriginal people weren't allowed to speak their language while white people were around. They had to go out into the bush to talk their lingoes on their own. Aboriginal customs like initiation were not allowed. We could not leave Cherbourg to go to Aboriginal traditional festivals. We could have a corroboree if the Protector issued a permit. It was completely up to him. I never had a chance to learn about my traditional and customary way of life.
> Confidential submission number 110.

> 'When I come back I couldn't even speak my own language. And that really buggered my identity up. It took me forty odd years before I became a man in my own people's eyes, through Aboriginal Law.'
> Confidential evidence number 179.

> 'Y'know, I can remember we used to just talk lingo. They used to tell us not to talk that language, that it's devil's language. And they'd wash our mouths with soap. We sorta had to sit down with Bible language all the time. So it sorta wiped out all our language that we knew.
> Confidential evidence number 170.

> '...when our children were stolen from our families one of the

things that happened was that the language learning cycles were broken. Transmission from generation to generation is a crucial link in language maintenance. Taking the children away broke this link.'

Confidential submission number 759.

'It was a crime to teach languages, that's why we were going backwards...The old people were frightened to teach us our language. It was fear.'

Quoted by Michael Aird in *'I Know a Few Words':Talking about Aboriginal Languages*, Keeaira Press, Southport, 1966.

'I could have at least had another language and been able to communicate with these people. You know I go there today and I have to communicate in English or use an interpreter. They're like my family, they're closer than any family I've got and I can't even talk to them.'

Confidential evidence number 313.

'We lost much of our culture, our language and traditional knowledge, our kinship and our land.'

Confidential evidence number 821.

'Language and identity are closely linked, and for many of us our language is a symbol of identity central to our self-esteem, cultural respect and social identification. Our languages provide more than just a way to talk to each other. They provide a way for us to interpret the reality we see around us. The words we use to name things, to describe feelings, understandings and each other, carry meanings particular to us. If we lose these words, we lose part of ourselves.'

Submitted by the Kimberley Language Resource Centre.

'What must be remembered is that language is not simply a

tool for everyday communication, but through recording of stories, songs, legends, poetry and lore, holds the key to a people's history and opens the door to cultural and spiritual understanding.'

Aboriginal and Torres Strait Islander Corporation of
Languages, submission number 854.

As an alien culture was forced upon them, the children had to follow the religion of that culture, sometimes in conditions of gross degradation, poverty and hunger.

'That's another thing—culture was really lost there, too. Because religion was drummed into us, y'know, when we'd be out there and we'd have knuckle-up and that, we were that religious we'd kneel down in prayer…We had to pray every time you swear or anything, you'd go down on your hands and knees…they pumped that religion into us.

'Night time we used to cry with hunger, y'know, lice, no food. And we used to go out there to the town dump…we had to come and scrounge at the dump, y'know, eating old bread and smashing tomato sauce bottles and licking them. Half of the time our food we got from the rubbish dump. Always hungry there.'

Confidential evidence number 549.

In their stories the stolen children frequently refer to the problems arising from the skin colour of people of mixed race. Some of the short anecdotes highlight these problems. When authorities came to take away the children with lighter skins, the mothers would attempt to disguise the children, blackening their bodies artificially.

'Every morning our people would crush charcoal and mix that with animal fat and smother that all over us, so that when the police came they could only see black children in the distance. We were told to be on the alert and, if white people came, to run into the bush or run and stand behind the trees as stiff as a poker, or else hide behind logs or run into culverts and hide. Often the white people—we didn't know who they were—would come into our camps. And if the Aboriginal group was taken unawares, they would stuff us into flour bags and pretend we weren't there. We were told not to sneeze. We knew if we sneezed and they knew we were in there bundled up, we'd be taken off and away from the area.'

Confidential evidence number 681.

You spend your whole life wondering where you fit. You're not white enough to be white and your skin isn't black enough to be black either, and it really does come down to that.'

Confidential evidence number 210.

'I felt like a stranger in Ernabella, a stranger in my father's people. We had no identity with the land, no identity with a certain people.

'I've decided in the last ten, eleven years to, y'know, I went through the law. I've been learning culture and learning everything that goes with it because I felt, growing up, that I wasn't really a blackfella. You hear whitefellas tell you you're a blackfella. But blackfellas tell you you're a whitefella. So you're caught in a half-caste world.'

Confidential evidence number 289.

There are frequent references to the shock that was delivered to a family when the authorities came and took the children, references to the bewilderment and powerlessness of the people.

Welfare just took the lot, no reason—just took us. They took mum and dad to court here for no reason. But there was no neglect. We was happy kids, you know. We just—we lived in the bush all our lives. Dad never believed in bringing his family to the city, he just loved the bush and that's where we stayed. We were always fed and happy there but I suppose they were looking for this other family and when they came to take them they just decided, Well we'll take these as well.'

Confidential evidence number 321.

'I was at the post office with my Mum and Auntie [and cousin]. They put us in the police ute and said they were taking us to Broome. They put the mums in there as well. But when we'd gone [about ten miles] they stopped and threw the mothers out of the car. We jumped on our mothers' backs, crying, trying not to be left behind. But the policeman pulled us off and threw us back in the car. When we got to Broome they put me and my cousin in the Broome lock-up. We were only ten years old. We were in the lock-up for two days waiting for the boat to Perth.'

Confidential evidence number 821.

'Mum was kidnapped. My grandfather was away working at the time, and he came home and found that his kids had been taken away, and he didn't know nothing about it. Four years later he died of a broken heart. He had a breakdown and was sent to Kew Hospital. He was buried in a pauper's grave and on his death certificate he died of malnutrition, ulcers and plus he had bedsores. He was fifty-one.'

Confidential evidence number 143.

'I grew up Oodnadatta area...with my grandmother and she would see the missionary coming...she would run away with me. She would keep running and the police...would come sometimes and shoot the dogs and that and my grandmother would run in the creek and hide me away till about really dark and come back home...I might [have] been about ten or eleven years...we seen one missionary coming...one of my auntie roll me up like a swag sort of thing, you know, and hid me away...but I must have moved and he got me out and he said to me, "I'll give you a lolly and we'll go for a ride, go to Oodnadatta"...they put me on a train and my grandmother was following the train—she was running behind the train, singing out for me...then I singing out, "I'll be back", I thought I was going for a holiday or something.

Confidential evidence number 382.

The 'split the litter' approach referred to by Penny in her story is frequently described in the anecdotes.

'I wasn't allowed to go to the same school where my natural siblings were attending school. I knew my siblings' names but I didn't know what they looked like. I was told not to contact my natural family...My foster family and the Welfare Officer said to me that I shouldn't get in touch with my natural family because they were not "any good".'

Confidential evidence number 314.

'The grief came for my younger sister and two brothers whom I thought I would never see again. The day I left the Orphanage— that was a very sad day for me. I was very unhappy, and the memories came back. There was nowhere to turn. You was on your own. I was again in a different environment...I had no choice but to stick it out. With the hardships going and thinking of my sister and brothers which I left at the Orphanage. My heart is full of sorrows for them.'

Confidential evidence number 681.

'One thing that really, really sticks in my mind is being put into this cold bed with white starchy sheets and having to sleep on my own and looking down the room and just seeing rows of beds and not knowing where my brothers and sister were.'

Confidential evidence number 227.

Although some of the Indigenous people speak of being loved and well-treated by the families who adopted them, they often repeat the fact that nothing can make up for the loss of their Indigenous identity. Another perspective is that of the people who adopted Indigenous children out of genuine compassion and love.

'I got everything that could reasonably be expected: a good home environment, education, stuff like that, but that's all material stuff. It's all the non-material stuff that I didn't have— the lineage. It's like you're the first human being at times. You know, you've just come out of nowhere; there you are. In terms of having a direction in life, how do you know where you're going if you don't know where you've come from?'

Confidential evidence number 136.

'...even though I had a good education with [adoptive family] and I went to college, there was just this feeling that I did not belong there. The best day of my life was when I met my brothers because I felt like I belonged and I finally had a family.'

Confidential evidence number 384.

'In 1960 my wife and I applied to adopt an Aboriginal baby, after reading in the newspapers that these babies were remaining in institutionalised care, going to orphanages, as no-one would adopt them. Later that year we were offered a baby who had been cared for since birth in a church-run babies' home in Brunswick. We were delighted! We had been told, and truly believed that his mother was dead and his father unknown. Where we lived there seemed to be no Aboriginals around. We knew some were grouped in Northcote and in Fitzroy but the stories told about them were so negative, we felt we should avoid them at least until Ken was much older. [By the time Ken was a teenager] he was in fact an isolated individual, alienated from the stream of life with no feeling for a past or a future, subject to racism in various forms day in and day out. No wonder he withdrew, and as he told me later, considered suicide on occasions. When Ken was eighteen he found his natural family, three sisters and a brother. His mother was no longer living. She died some years earlier when Ken was four. Because of the long timespan, strong bonds with his family members could not be established.'

Confidential evidence number 266.

Throughout the stories, short and long, there is a constant reference to the loss of tribal identity and place, the loss of soul and the loss of country.

'My grandparents waited for me to come home and I never came home. My grandfather died in 1978 and my grandmother died in 1979. I came home in 1980.'

Confidential evidence number 522.

These voices and all the others of the stolen generations insist on a hearing, on understanding, and on response.

Perspectives

BRINGING THEM HOME WAS tabled in the House of Representatives and in the Senate on 27 May 1997. Of the many perspectives taken by Australians who read the Report, the following is a selection of some reactions to the stories of the stolen children, both within the Parliament and in the community. Just as I hope that in collecting the stories of the stolen children I may inspire more people to read the whole text of *Bringing Them Home*, in quoting some edited sections from the parliamentary debates at the time of the Report, I hope that people may be moved to examine the full texts of those debates in the cause of understanding, reconciliation and apology. By publishing a small selection of other responses, I offer a range of approaches to the issue of the stolen children.

As I said in the Introduction, the narrative of the public response to the stories of the stolen generations has developed and moved on over the time it has taken for me to compile this book. As a consequence, some of the documents collected here have acquired the flavour of history, and the events described in them have been followed by certain changes and results. Sometimes I have even been visited by the idea that by the time this book was finished, the Prime Minister might have apologised to Indigenous people on behalf of the rest of the nation.

I

John Howard

Prime Minister of Australia

I HAVE SAID REPEATEDLY that anybody who argues that Aboriginal and Torres Strait Islander people are not as a group more profoundly disadvantaged than other sections of the Australian community are flying in the face of reality. People who argue that are substituting fiction for fact. They are substituting selective anecdotes for irrefutable statistical proof and they are also ignoring the realities that are around us to see.

[...]

We are not obsessed with symbolism. We are concerned, though, with practical outcomes.

[...]

I feel a very deep sorrow for indigenous people who suffered under the injustices of policies pursued by past generations. I think all members of the House can understand the pain and trauma that many of the people who were affected by those practices might continue to suffer. Rather than reducing the quality of a nation, I think that it enhances the quality of a nation for all of us to recognise that people affected by such policies did suffer pain, did suffer injustice, do continue to be affected by it and have had their lives affected by it in a very significant way.

The government has indicated in the submission that it made to the royal commission that it did not believe that financial compensation was appropriate. That is an issue that will be dealt with in more detail when the comprehensive response of the government is brought forward to this parliament. I said also at the reconciliation convention yesterday that I did not believe that current generations of Australians could be held accountable for or regarded as guilty for the acts of earlier generations over which they had no control.

I do not believe that, as a community, we can ignore history. We must openly acknowledge the injustices of the past. As an intensely proud Australian, along, I am sure, with all other Australians who have a balanced view of the history of this country, I am immensely proud of what we have achieved over the last two hundred years. I believe that the Australian achievement is something of which all of us should be proud. It has been a heroic achievement in the face of immense difficulties.

That does not gainsay the fact that there have been significant blemishes. Undoubtedly, the most significant blemish of all in the history of this country over the last two hundred years has been the treatment of our indigenous people. I would have thought that was an unarguable fact. I would have thought it was a concept that all of us could embrace, but I would have thought that we could have embraced it without developing an approach to reconciliation that looks backwards rather than forward.

I believe that the proper basis of reconciliation is to recognise the truth about the past, to remain proud about what this country has achieved during the years of its existence, and to resolve, united together as Australians, to work towards a better and more cooperative future. The most effective way of doing that and the most effective way in which we can honour the passage of the 1967 referendum [The people of Australia made a judgement in 1967 that the then existing arrangements to assist Aboriginal and Torres Strait Islander people were not working effectively and that they could only be made to work more effectively if the Commonwealth Parliament were given the power] and the wisdom of the Australian people expressed with that referendum is to commit our energy, our resources and our time to remedying those areas of continuing disadvantage amongst the most disadvantaged group within our Community—the Aboriginal and Torres Strait Islander people.

(From Hansard, 27 May 1997)

2

Kim Beazley

Leader of the Opposition

i) [...] THE PRIME MINISTER SAID that we ought to focus on the future and that we ought to focus upon, primarily, the physical and educational needs of the Aboriginal people. Of course we must focus on all those things. Of course those issues are central. Of course the educational and health needs of the Aboriginal population are absolutely central to the day-to-day concerns of the government. There is no question about that. We would question whether or not this government's commitment to that has been adequate, but we would not question the principle of it.

There are also symbolic issues. There are also issues which go to the sense in the Aboriginal community of their place in the Australian political system, which issues are critical as well. They are a people of nations who live by symbols. They are a people of nations who live by gestures. They are a people who are actually an extraordinarily forgiving people if the symbols are acknowledged. They will allow an issue to pass where they get that recognition because they are a people of the spirit as much as they are a people of physical nature.

These things are therefore worth concentrating on and being concerned with as we sit down to think these issues through. They are not people to be toyed with politically in an Australian domestic context; they have been toyed with for a very long time and they do not deserve that. They are not people of substantial power in the community; they are not people to be feared. They are people to be treasured, and that is something that really ought to be reflected in the resolutions of this parliament.

[...]

We will have an opportunity to make restitution. We will have an opportunity to state generously what we believe about the nature of race relations in this country. We will have an opportunity in that regard to make the national apology that needs to be made at that point of time for the suffering of those people who have experienced such an extraordinary deprivation as a result of quite recent government decisions, both state and federal. We will have a chance for a bit of an outpouring of emotion in this parliament in a way in which there ought to be at that point in time.

(From Hansard, House of Representatives, 27 May 1997)

ii) I had an opportunity to read a fair proportion of this Report [*Bringing Them Home*] last night, and one thing is amply clear to me. As I read through that Report, the materials contained within it refer to operations that occurred when the Labor party was in office.

For those things that we are responsible for, I apologise, as Leader of the Australian Labor Party. This is a terrible, terrible record. This record does not deal with the experience of Aboriginals in good-hearted homes with kindly foster parents. There may be some reference to that and the consequences of that, which of course were the consequences which were the least difficult to bear for the Aboriginal people. Many very decent people took up that fostering status, and they did so without maliciousness and with the very best intentions. This Report is not really about them. That is the truth of the matter.

It does refer to them of course in the context of the extent to which those people nevertheless, without knowing it, were implicated in a deculturalisation of a race, with all the loss of identity that flowed from that and the extraordinary difficulties that they confronted. However, what the Report does detail is very different experiences, experiences of viciousness of extraordinary dimensions—experiences of sexual assault, of physical assault, of overt pressured propagandisation.

This is not a matter that we can sweep under the table. This not a matter that we can stand aside from. This is not a matter about which I direct blame at this government. It is not a matter about which I would believe that I am in any moral position to do so, and that is not what my intention is here today.

My intention is to try to provide this parliament with an opportunity that the Western Australian parliament, under Richard Court—of all people—and the South Australian government, under John Olsen, took without any blush, without any concern for their reputations and without any worry about what might be the legal implications of what they said. They decided that they would stand in their parliaments and apologise; they would stand in their parliaments and make a statement about what their intentions were. This is what we believed that we would have an opportunity to discuss here today. We have not.

[...]

Why should not the Aboriginal people of this nation be accorded equality? Why not? Why not let the Aboriginal people of this nation have the same experience and the same access? When, for malicious reasons or non-malicious reasons, deep personal damage is done to you, you have recourse. Why not? Why should that not happen? Why are they not people who are at least equal to us in the opportunities that are available to them?

That is not an easy process to contemplate. I was going to read some of these cases, but I cannot. I was pretty late going through it—and this would have been a better speech if I had not.

Mr. Speaker, you cannot walk away from them. This chamber cannot walk away from them. The government cannot walk away from them. They have to be confronted. There are processes by which you can do that. You can do it the easy way, or you can do it the hard way. The easy way is to allow a motion to proceed to make the first step of restitution: that is the apology. That is the part of the easy way. The second part of the easy way is for the Commonwealth to engage the states in a conversation as to how they will handle it. The third part of the easy way is to deal with this, possibly, in the way in which the land fund has been dealt with—there is an opportunity not to do the compensation on budget, but to draw down from it from time to time. The fourth part of the easy way is to get a formula in place, as suggested at length in this Report, whereby, for various types of problems, people's situations are assessed and dealt with. That is the easy way.

The hard way is this: ignore it and let those compensation cases roll through the court with every piece of disturbance in race relations in this country that follows as, one after another, the courts compensate Aboriginal people for the wrongs done to them. That is the hard way; it is the divisive way in the community.

I urge the Prime Minister [Mr. Howard] to seize this opportunity now and take the easy way for all of us, and to reach a conclusion on this that will ensure that this parliament performs its responsibilities for an apology, and that this parliament performs its responsibilities for restitution. It is a situation that lies in his hands and cries out for leadership—he must provide it.

3

Senator Crowley

Labor Senator for South Australia

I RISE TO SPEAK tonight on the *Bringing Them Home* Report of the national inquiry into the separation of Aboriginal and Torres Strait Islander children from their families. I suppose everyone is going to say something of the impact of this Report on them, but tonight I thought I would tell just some of the impact of this Report on me. I opened the front cover of the Report and read:

> 'This Report is a tribute to the strength and struggles of many thousands of Aboriginal and Torres Strait Islander people affected by forcible removal. We acknowledge the hardships they endured and the sacrifices they made. We remember and lament all the children who will never come home.'

Another paragraph does follow, but I wanted to add another line that says: 'We remember all the mothers with a great gap, and aching heart and empty arms that could never embrace their children—those children who never came home.' If ever there were a report to break the hearts of people, it is this one; if ever there were a report that lists the broken hearts of thousands of women, of thousands of families, it is this one.

I believe that this is an absolute watershed report—an extraordinary, significant, amazing 700 page Report. I certainly want to congratulate and acknowledge the producers of this Report, from President Ronald Wilson to all of the members of the committee, who listened to the testimony that is listed in such detail and in such generosity in the pages of this Report.

This 700 page Report is full of pain. The words that occur again and again are sad, sad, sad. The Report to the extent that I have been able to read it seems to me to be almost entirely lacking rancour. It is lacking anger. It is just full of sadness.

[...]

For me the 1970s is not a very long time ago. I find it absolutely shocking to read these stories and to somehow know that, while I did not know as a child, I had a faint idea, I suppose, as a doctor in South Australia in the 1960s. I was certainly assisted in this matter because I had a brother who worked with Aboriginal people for many years, so perhaps I had access to closer information. But even so I had no idea that we were talking about the history of a planned campaign—and I do think genocide is the right word—to eliminate a race from the face of the earth, that those people were actually having this kind of pain and anguish visited upon them right alongside of us.

[...]

I do urge everyone who can to read this Report and to just think about what sort of pain this history shows, what it says about us as a race and why I believe it is critically important that we as a nation, let alone as individuals, apologise. I so do.

(From Hansard, Senate, 28 May 1997)

In the Senate on 29 May 1997, Senator Rosemary Crowley spoke about the Report, making a passionate and personal response. After expressing her particular impressions and perspectives, Senator Crowley apologised to the stolen generations.

4

Lang Dean

MY FATHER WAS A Victorian policeman from 1922 until 1946. He spent a long spell of duty at Echuca and he was there when the Deniliquin and Balranald railway spurs were constructed.

The rail workers came to Echuca to spend their earnings and let off steam. My father made 343 arrests on average in those years. He was a good and conscientious policeman. During 1937–1938, when I was seven or eight years old, he would some-times come off duty and, as was his custom, sit on a stool outside our kitchen and take his helmet off. On occasions he would be crying and sobbing like a child, I would be upset to see such a strong man cry and ask him why. He said he would not tell me as I was too young to understand but he would tell me when I grew up. What he did say then was: 'Son, don't ever be a policeman, it's a dirty job.'

After he left the force, when I was about 16 years old, he and I were camping on a fishing trip and we were sitting around the campfire. I had often thought about how Dad cried years ago so I asked him would he tell me the reason. He told me that when he went on duty those mornings his sergeant would order him to accompany two welfare officers to Cumragunga, a mission station, to give them bodily protection when they entered nice clean simple homes of half-caste people and bodily removed nine, ten, eleven and twelve year-old children from loving mothers and fathers into commandeered taxis. They were then taken to the Echuca railway station and sent to the far reaches of NSW and Queensland. They were farmed out to service to wealthy business-men and graziers. No doubt a few were treated well but the rest would be thrown on the human scrap-heap when finished with.

So that was the reason my father cried on those days.

Ms Hanson, Mr Fischer and Mr Howard, when you kneel down to say your prayers tonight, thank God you don't have a burly policeman and two welfare officers on you doorstep in the morning to take your children away.

(First published as a letter to the editor in *The Age*,
24 May 1997)

5

Marilyn Lake

Professor in History at La Trobe University

IN THE PASSIONATE DEBATE around the release of the Stolen Generations Report, some conservatives have said that we should not judge the past by today's standards.

Acting Prime Minister Tim Fischer, for example, has said that the government officials and missionaries who helped to remove part-Aboriginal children from their mothers believed at the time that they were doing the right thing.

The response implies that although we now recognise the child removal policy to have been misguided, in the past there was agreement on what were the best interests of the child. Everyone of that time agreed, the argument runs, that it was better for Aboriginal and mixed descent children to be raised in white homes and institutions.

Yet the argument assumes a past consensus where there was none. The policy of child removal was contested at the time, while it was going on.

The historical record documents vocal public opposition to the removal of children. In the 1930s a leading critic, Mary Bennett, described the policy as the 'official smashing of family life'.

Much of the criticism came from feminists engaged in missionary work. Bennett, perhaps the period's most persistent white advocate of Aboriginal rights, taught from 1932 at the Mt Margaret Mission in Western Australia.

Who would disagree, then or now, with Bennett's sentiment that 'no department in the world can take the place of a child's mother'? But it is not surprising that so little is known about this political activism today, because for the most part the campaigns belong to the political history of women, a history that has largely languished in obscurity.

Feminist organisations between the wars were centrally concerned with improving the status and rights of all mothers.

Bennett and other feminists worked through organisations such as the Australian Federation of Women Voters, the Woman's Christian Temperance Union and the London-based women's rights group, the British Commonwealth League—to which Bennett's paper on The Aboriginal Mother in Western Australia was read in 1933.

In Western Australia in 1934 feminists formed a political alliance with Aboriginal women to present evidence to a Royal Commission—created largely in response to feminist agitation— to 'Investigate, Report and Advise upon Matters in relation to the Condition and Treatment of Aborigines'.

At the hearings, Aboriginal women told of the brutal treatment, including flogging, they had suffered at the government settlement at Moore River. Others told of the pain involved in being separated from their children. 'I want to know,' said Mary Nannup, 'the reason for my children being taken from me.'

Feminist witnesses supported Aboriginal women in their claims to the rights of custody and maintenance. Observing that it had become 'more or less the practice to take the children away', Ada Bromham said the law had to be amended to give Aboriginal mothers legal rights over their children. The dependence of feminist witnesses on Aboriginal women's accounts led to them being admonished by Royal Commissioner Moseley for offering only 'hearsay...interesting, but valueless'.

When asked whether it was not better for neglected children to be removed from their families, Bessie Rischbieth, president of the

Australian Federation of Women Voters, insisted that 'in most instances I should prefer to see the children left with their parents...and that the system of dealing with the parents should be improved in order that they might keep their children'.

But it was Bennett who was most eloquent in her denunciation of government policy. She spoke of the lives of terror led by the hunted ones:

'So mothers with infants and individual children and some-times families are mustered up like cattle and deported to the remote Government native settlement at Moore River, there to drag out their days and years in exile, suffering all the miseries of transportation for no fault, but only because the white supplanters are too greedy and too mean to give them living areas...They are captured at all ages, as infants in arms...they are not safe until they are dead.'

Feminist opposition to the government policy of removing part-Aboriginal children was an extension of the maternalism that characterised feminist political thought in those years. Maternalists saw the task of government as providing care to the vulnerable and defenceless; they also focused on the mother as the national political figure around whom they mobilised.

While feminists were effective in drawing attention to the appalling consequences of taking children away, they were unsuc-cessful in effecting a change in policy.

Feminist arguments about the importance of mother love and Aboriginal people's relationships to country and family were no match for the experiment of 'biological absorption' propounded by Chief Protector A.O. Neville. At the Royal Commission, Bennett confessed to Neville that she saw him as an 'oppressor'; he taunted her with being an 'idealist'. 'I wish to treat other people as human beings,' she replied. 'I do not put it higher than that.'

Bennett was posing a challenge to her contemporaries, remind-
ing them that they did have a choice. Her statement is a challenge
to our contemporaries. They too, must decide what to do.

(From *The Age* 17, January 1998)

6

Senator Herron

Federal Minister for Aboriginal and
Torres Strait Islander Affairs

[...]

THE REPORT IS A very detailed and lengthy document of almost 700 pages canvassing a wide range of issues. I would like to say at the outset that the Report catalogues what can only be described as a sad and tragic episode in Australia's history. I myself had commented earlier that it was horrific.

As I have said before, anyone wanting to understand aspects of the indigenous experience and some of its contemporary characteristics would be well advised to read some of the individual case histories and evidence produced in the Report.

Much discussion in recent days has focused on the question of an apology for the events recorded in the Report. The Prime Minister [Mr Howard], the Governor-General and myself have expressed our feelings in this respect. It should be noted that the main focus of the Report is on how governments should deal with the continuing effects of past policies in terms of the family reunion and related services and on current policy and practices.

The government acknowledges the impact of these past policies and practices and is already working to address the significant disadvantage currently being experienced by all Aboriginal and Torres Strait Islander peoples.

The Report's recommendations can be broadly grouped into three categories: firstly, reparation or compensation for the individuals, their families, communities and descendants; secondly, reunion, health and other services for those affected by past policies and practices; and, thirdly, Commonwealth legislation to regulate current state and territory child welfare adoption and juvenile justice practices and to enable transfer of jurisdiction to indigenous organisations as a form of self-government.

[...]

At the Commonwealth level we will need to give careful consideration to those recommendations which suggest action on the part of the Commonwealth. As I have already made clear, the government is committed to developing a practical response based on a commonsense approach that addresses the present and the future.

[...]

Finally I would acknowledge that this is a very emotional and important issue, not just for indigenous Australians but for all Australians. It is about heart and soul and family. I would hope that we, as members of the national parliament, can take a constructive and mature approach to this issue. That means a calm and sensible consideration of the Report and its recommendations and a commitment to seek a practical and realistic response.

(From Hansard, Senate, 28 May 1997)

7

Robert Manne

Associate Professor of Politics at La Trobe University

i) FROM THE LATE 19TH century to the 1960s Australian governments, as a practice and a policy, removed part-Aboriginal mothers, families and communities, often by force. The children were placed in institutions. In many cases physical mistreatment, sexual exploitation and extreme forms of moral humiliation occurred. No one knows exactly how many children were removed. All that one can say for certain is that tens of thousands were involved and that for very many an intense pain of abandonment and loss blighted their lives.

Five weeks ago Senator John Herron on behalf of the Prime Minister, wrote to Father Frank Brennan on the 'stolen generations'. His letter made clear, for the first time officially so far as I know, the Government's unwillingness to offer a formal apology. Senator Herron explained the decision thus: 'Such an apology could imply that present generations are in some way responsible and accountable for the actions of earlier generations, actions that were sanctioned by the laws of the time, and that were believed to be in the best interests of the children concerned.' One half of Senator Herron's justification for the unwillingness of his Government to apologise is trivial. It may be true that the policies of child removal were authorised under law. However, it is obviously not the legality but the morality of these acts which is in question.

The other half—the good intentions defence—seems more

serious. Yet it relies on the belief that a policy may be justified on the grounds of its good intentions so long as the policy-makers assure us that their intentions were good.

Such an argument can be disposed of quickly. When the Nazis, to take an extreme example, decided to rid the earth of the Jews the chief executors of the 'final solution' argued the goodness of their intentions. The Jews befouled the world. Their extermination would free the earth from their corrupting presence. What this example shows is that for a policy to be defended on the grounds of its good intentions, such intentions must be recognisable to us as good.

The question, then, is whether there exists a way in which the policy of child removal may well be plausibly construed as well intentioned.

Many Australians, including John Howard, think there is. What they believe is that the part-Aboriginal children were removed for what might be called social welfare reasons, because the particular children were assessed as being in danger.

This line of defence lies at the core of the present confusion over the stolen children. For while it must, of course, have been true that some of the children were in danger of harm, it is absolutely false to claim that the motives of those who removed them were of a social-welfarist kind. They were driven by altogether different motives.

The policy and practice of child removal was, at its heart, the response of Australian governments to a 'problem' that stirred public opinion and politicians alike—especially before 1950—the problem of the so-called half-caste.

European Australians thought of the children born of sexual encounters between European or Chinese makes and Aboriginal women, and of their descendents—whom they labelled, almost zoologically, as cross-breeds, quadroons, octoroons—as a growing and fearful social problem and with an undisguised cultural contempt.

The Perth *Sunday Times* in 1927 put it thus: 'Central Australia's half-caste problem...must be tackled boldly and immediately. The greatest danger, experts agree, is that three races will develop in Australia—white, black, and the pathetic sinister third race which is neither.'

To perceive of a group of human beings as a 'problem' is, of course, to hanker after a 'solution'. The most important solution to the problem posed by 'the half-caste' to the purity of White Australia was the policy of child removal. By seizing children of mixed descent, institutionalising them, teaching them to despise their Aboriginal inheritance and sending them out to work as station hands or domestic servants, authorities wanted to sever the cultural connection between the children of mixed descent and their Aboriginal families and communities and to prepare them for a place in the lower strata of European society.

Some Aboriginal administrators, in the interwar period, went further. They concocted a eugenics policy for 'breeding out the colour' of the part Aborigines, a policy known as biological assimilation. Such a policy involved not only the forceable separation of children from their mothers but also attempts at state control over marriage patterns. In Western Australia laws were passed in 1936 giving the Chief Protector of Aborigines, A.O. Neville, near-complete control over the lives of all Aborigines up to the age of 21, including the capacity to encourage marriages between 'half-caste' females and European males and to all but prohibit marriages between 'half-castes' and 'full-bloods'.

As Neville believed that in the fullness of time the full-blood Aborigines would be extinct, he dreamt that his policies of 'breeding out the color' would lead, eventually, to an Aborigine-free Australia. In April 1937, he placed before his colleagues at the first national governmental conference on Aborigines the following question: 'Are we going to have a population of 1,000,000 blacks in the Commonwealth, or are we going to merge them into our white community and eventually forget that there were any Aborigines in Australia?'

Such a policy seems to me the most shameful act in 20th-century Australia. Now that the facts are, belatedly, known, the Howard Government's refusal to apologise to its victims has extended to our generation the original shame.

ii) I am sure that I am not the only person who has been struck by how confused the Howard Government has been in its attempts to explain why it cannot apologise over the barbarous, long-term government practice of removing part-Aboriginal children from their families.

Mr. Howard began by telling us that his government could not apologise because it represented not only Anglo-Celtic Australians but also those citizens of non-English-speaking background, who had no personal responsibility for the past policies of Aboriginal child removal.

What did he mean? As the vast majority of Anglo-Celtic Australians, including everyone under 40, are in no way responsible for such policies, Mr. Howard's words somehow suggested that 'migrants' were less truly involved in the history of Australia than Anglo-Celts. Such thinking was common in Australia before the 1970s. It is odd to find Mr. Howard echoing such a view today.

Yet Mr. Howard's confusion does not end here. Because migrants cannot be held personally responsible, Mr. Howard thinks it inappropriate for his Government to offer a national apology. Yet he is happy to offer a private apology on his own behalf.

So far as I know, Mr. Howard was never personally implicated in the design or implemention of the child-removal policies. If the absence of certain citizens' direct responsibility for such policies prevents his Government from offering an apology, why doesn't a similar absence in his own case render a personal apology meaningless? And why does Mr. Howard not understand that in the matter of the stolen children his private apology has no more value than the apology of any citizen, and that it is solely in his capacity as Prime Minister that we are interested in his willingness to offer an apology?

Here Mr Howard stands firm. The Australian Government will not apologise. For such an apology might imply that 'the present generations are in some way responsible and accountable for the actions of earlier generations'. This statement takes us to the heart of Mr. Howard's confusion—his misunderstanding of the kind of relationship that exists between the present generation of Australians and the country's past.

To be fair, Mr. Howard's view is rooted in half-truth. Without their personal participation individuals do not bear guilt for shameful episodes in their country's history. On the other hand because we are not only individuals but also members of a nation, and because we live not only in the present but within a historical continuum, where the past has shaped the present and where what we make of this past will help shape the future, we are all deeply implicated in the history of our nation. It is not as individuals but as members of the nation, the 'imagined community', that the present generation has indeed inherited a responsibility for this country's past.

Australians have always had good reason to feel pride in aspects of their past—the pioneering tradition, the egalitarian ethos, the sustained civic peace, the wonderful success of post-war migration. Yet, increasingly, over the past 30 years, many Australians, in whom their country's history is alive, have come to see that there is one dimension of this history—the destruction of Aboriginal society in the 19th century and its terrible aftermath in the 20th— that is unambiguously dark.

Nothing, in my opinion, goes deeper in the psyche of contemporary Australia; nothing bears within itself more hope for the future than the present coming to terms with what the Governor-

General, Sir William Deane, once called our 'legacy of unutterable shame'.

Many Australians are now involved in a process we have come to call 'reconciliation'. This is a two-way process. It asks of non-indigenous Australians that we find ways of expressing our shame at the hand Aborigines have been dealt over time. Yet it asks of indigenous Australian far more—that, having observed such expressions, they find it in their hearts to forgive.

It was only in the past year or so that most non-indigenous Australians learnt about one particular troubling aspect of this past—that for the first 70 years of this century tens of thousands of part-Aboriginal babies and children were routinely, systematically, even casually, taken from their mothers and families by governmental officials and placed in institutions or foster homes. The motives for such a policy might have been complex and mixed. None the less it is genuinely difficult to imagine a non-violent policy more cruel than the severing of the spiritual and biological link between mother and child, or more expressive of racist contempt for the humanity and human rights of Australia's Aborigines.

Earlier this year *Bringing Them Home*, the Report of the Human Rights and Equal Opportunity Commission into the question of the stolen children, was published. It called on the Howard Government to issue a formal apology on our behalf. Shortly after its publication, the most important reconciliation conference in Australia's history took place. Some believed that a solemn government apology at this conference might have marked a true moral turning point. As we all know it was not to be.

Last week when the refusal of the Howard Government to apologise was finally formalised, the new head of the Council for Aboriginal Reconciliation, Evelyn Scott, advised fellow Aboriginal leaders to abandon finally their political campaign to secure a Government apology over the question of the stolen children. In my opinion her advice was wise.

In the absence of what she called 'a generous and genuine spirit', an apology forcefully extracted, like a rotten tooth, from a grudging government, blind to the moral meaning of its words and fearful of their financial cost, would be worse than useless.

Perhaps having relinquished the editorship of *Quadrant* to P.P. McGuinness, a man who regards the question of an apology to the stolen children as 'pharisaical breast beating' and as an exercise in New Class 'thought control', I am unduly gloomy. But the episode of the non-apology has convinced me at least of one thing. In contemporary Australia the hope of reconciliation remains still a distant dream.

(This piece appeared in *The Age* and the *Sydney Morning Herald* in two parts, on the first and 22 December 1997. Robert Manne is the former editor of *Quadrant*. A selection of his essays and journalism will be published in 1998.)

8

Jack Waterford

Editor of the Canberra Times

JOHN HOWARD IS NOT the only person who is not listening in Aboriginal affairs, even if he has shamed and enraged many Australians by his mean-minded failure to make an unequivocal apology to the Aboriginal stolen children. There is not much sign that the other side is listening either.

The Reconciliation conference was potentially a defining moment in black and white relations, but given the apparent attitude that all of the concessions and gestures must come from government, it was always unlikely that there would be a meeting of minds. Howard might still have had the grace to mouth some uniting words of regret. It is not even unfair to imagine that he, as he hectored the conference, was consciously speaking to a constituency which has been listening too much to Pauline Hanson.

The fact is that the Howard Government does not care a lot about appeasing current Aboriginal leaders, or in indulging their agendas. He will not be blackmailed by any choruses from international voices or ecclesiastics either. It is not just stubbornness, sheer bastardry, or a serious Hanson agenda to complete the dispossession of Aborigines. He is playing a different game, one which involves his desire to destroy a political establishment and a framework of thinking created by his opponents in politics. Aborigines ought now be calculating whether engaging Howard in what he would regard as set-ups is more profitable than some active engagement to get what can be got.

At the moment, for example, the litmus tests for the Government are apparently its approaches to the Wik legislation and to the stolen children. Neither were particularly strong issues only seven months ago. Until the High Court's Wik decision, few Aborigines were confident that the litigation would open any doors at all. Personally, I am very sceptical about whether any were opened at all, even assuming that the Government would not effectively override it. Most Aborigines will not be affected in any way because they never had any opportunities for claims under Wik (or Mabo, for that matter either).

The stolen children inquiry has been around for some time, and perhaps its most important work was in its evidence-gathering phase, in its giving the victims their first platforms not only to speak of their pain and their dispossession but to lay bare a policy which was conceived to break up Aboriginality.

Those who set up the inquiry saw the importance of revelation, acknowledgement and reconciliation, but what has been on some people's minds—questions of individual compensation—has never been on the wider political agenda. Were it so, many ordinary people who were appalled at Howard's response to the inquiry, would still have many questions and end up on his side of the analysis.

The point is that the Government's approach to such issues is powerfully symbolic of its broader approach to Aboriginal affairs. Symbolism does matter. The signals which government has sent, non-stop since being elected, have been almost invariably appalling. But there is something too in Howard's words at the conference about reconciliation not working if it puts a higher priority on symbolic gestures and overblown rhetoric than the practical needs of Aboriginal Australians in areas like health, housing, education and employment.

One of the reasons why is that Aboriginal affairs have persist-
ently foundered by there being too many eggs in one basket. That
basket has often been not much more than a slogan—land rights,
or self-management, or reconciliation or whatever. At best they
have set up hopes which are almost bound to be dashed—by
Labor politicians as well as Liberal ones. At worst they distract
attention from the genuine political framework in Aboriginal
affairs in which the social and political interests of Aboriginal
Australians are brokered rather than begged, dispensed or
dispensed with.

The time is right for a radical rethinking of a lot of policies in
Aboriginal affairs, and it might lead to some accommodations
with an indifferent Howard. No one knows the need for such a
rethinking better than those who suffer from what is happening
and what has been happening over the past fifteen years. Inside
Aboriginal Australia there is plenty of criticism of the structure of
organisations, of the way services are being delivered, and plenty
of ideas about how things might change for the better. While
there might be plenty of criticism of government, there is ample
awareness that the basis for real change, and for any real liberation
from mendicancy, lies with Aboriginal communities and
organisations themselves. Some of the analysis and some of the
ideas would strike deep chords within the present government, if
only the two sides would speak honestly to each other.

It is quite easy to understand the suspicions of the Aboriginal
side. The Government has pandered to prejudice and misinfor-
mation in the community. The struggle is seen as saving what one
has rather than achieving more. The dialogue between the
leaderships is more focused on restatements of attitudes and
resentments, and, often on vilifying each other.

But there is not going to be any breathing space. The Government is not going to bow under the weight of the sermons or the
editorials, and cravenly admit it was completely wrong and hand
everything back. Aborigines will not discover that the Howard

Government was just an unpleasant interlude before Labor was restored and heaven returned to earth again so that we could all have more of the same which has brought us to the pretty pass. The Senate, or other devices, can make no effective difference either. It would be nice if the symbols were right and if more than lip service were paid both to reconciliation and a sense of partnership, but it takes two sides to do that.

When I think of the stolen generations, I think not only of the pain of those separated from their kin, but of the lives which have been wasted as Aboriginal affairs have failed to progress. After all of the hopes of three decades ago, there has been a new generation, white as well as black, who have encountered mostly frustration and despair—a time that was taken from them. If everyone does not get a bit practical there will be yet another one.

(From *Eureka Street*, July/August 1997.)

Senator Bob Brown

Australian Greens Senator for Tasmania

I ADD UNRESERVEDLY FROM the Australian Greens an apology to the Aboriginal people and, in particular, to those directly and indirectly affected as the stolen generations. There is no way we can express the awful tragedy at an individual and community level this policy wrought upon the indigenous peoples of this country. There is now an opportunity for us to reconsider and move into the future with an open heart and with the recognition that that past should never again be allowed. The way we can ensure that that past never be allowed again is by continually revisiting it as part of our history, as part of Australian history, that can never again be submerged.

The stolen generation's saga affects every corner of this country. It affects the Aboriginal people of Tasmania as it affects the Aboriginal people elsewhere around the country. We must move beyond the period of apology, if we get there—and that is an apology unreservedly required from the elected leader of this nation, the Prime Minister [Mr Howard], on behalf of the nation, to reparations as yet to be determined. It is a task for us all to undertake toward a future in which we draw strength from the unity and diversity of this nation and from the enormous wealth of this nation's indigenous peoples and their culture, and their affinity for the vast lands of Australia.

It is imperative that we make that journey. On Monday, a great opportunity was blighted by the cavilling and conditional words of the Prime Minister. It was a moment of potential, positive, historic land marking. It was a moment that was failed by the Prime Minister. It is an opportunity that rarely comes but, nevertheless, as he will know from the response he has had nationally and not just from the meeting in Melbourne, it is incumbent on him now to find the opportunity in the near future to do what he failed to do adequately on Monday. I will be amongst the many millions of other Australians who will support him, if he rises to that moment in the near future.

[...]

It is important that we move to heal as best we can so this country can move forward united and proud of the path we have put a light on into the next century.

(From Hansard, Senate, 28 May 1997.)

10

Graeme Campbell

Independent Federal Member for Kalgoorlie

I RISE TO SPEAK on the Report by Sir Ronald Wilson, as this is the first opportunity I have had to do so. My starting point for deliberation of this Report is that the author tells us that it is not an 'intellectual document'; it is 'from the heart'. What this means, of course, is that the Report is not constrained by fact or by evidence. In passing, it must be said that such a base is not an appropriate methodology for any government consideration or the running of a country.

The Report is also greatly flawed in other ways. For instance, Ronald Wilson seems mainly to have interviewed the clients who were sent to him by the Aboriginal Legal Service, and he has made no attempt to interview those people who refused to testify because they knew in their case it was the act of being taken away that saved their lives.

It is always easy on an issue such as this to trot out the highly emotional examples [...]

I remember the recent words of Isobel Lynnot who is now ninety-five years old. She along with her sister, were the first children to be taken to Beagle Bay, a Catholic mission, in 1909. Isobel's father was white and, when he died, her mother implored the local police officer to take her children as they would otherwise 'surely die'. Isobel remembers Beagle Bay very warmly. 'The nuns were very good to us,' she said. 'They gave us clean clothes, taught us to read and write and to play musical instruments. They taught us to sew and to dance.' She has only gratitude for her deliverance.

(From Hansard, House of Representatives, 28 May 1997)

11

Robert Sercombe

Labor Federal Member for Maribyrnong

I RISE FOLLOWING THE contribution of the member for Kalgoorlie [Mr Campbell] at this stage more in sorrow than in anger that a representative of the Australian people could be so unfeeling in the way in which he has responded to the Report produced by Sir Ronaldd Wilson. To suggest that the Report is not supported by fact and evidence is clearly sheer nonsense.

Mr Speaker, lest it be thought that we are talking about times long in the past or times long distant, let me refer to a few of the cases that were produced as evidence in the Report that comes from your and my home state of Victoria. In fact some of them come from the leafy suburbs of Balwyn, Blackburn South and Kew. [The case of Paul, detailed in 'The Stories', is cited here, along with other cases of recent origin.] They are situations where, in the words of Sir William Deane, [...] we as Australians ought to feel 'unutterable shame' in the dealings with our Aboriginal citizens.

I believe this Report to parliament ought to be dealt with against that background. It is an emotional debate. The issues are highly emotionally charged. But they deserve the detailed attention of this country in order for this country to really fulfil its potential of being a great and truly just nation.

(From Hansard, House of Representatives, 28 May 1997)

12

Martin Flanagan

Brother

I'M AN AUSTRALIAN. I haven't always known what the word meant. I grew up in Tasmania in a time when no-one talked about the past, neither the Aboriginal past nor the convict past from which I am descended. In the end, I thought I must be Irish. I went to that country and found I wasn't. For the next two years, I wandered the world wondering if I was actually from anywhere.

In the early '90s, I wrote a novel about that period of my life called *Going Away*. Basically, it was about how I began to understand what it means to be Australian. In the middle of the writing, the book crashed, as books sometimes do, so I went and saw an artist I admired, by name of Archie Roach. What do you do when your art stops moving, I asked. Follow my heart, he replied. So I did. When the book was published in 1993, a Sydney critic said it was a collection of stories which added up to nothing. Again I went and saw Archie. I had dedicated my book to him and conservationist Bob Brown, and I asked him to write something in the front of my copy. He reflected, looking off into the distance as he does, and wrote, 'To lose yourself, to find yourself, so see yourself anew—that is the journey. To my brother Martin, from Archie Roach.' I read it and thought, yes, that is what I believe.

I first saw Archie at a Paul Kelly concert at the Victorian Arts Centre in the mid '80s. A lot of guff is written about theatre being brave and daring when it's really more of the same. What happened that night was truly daring. The audience was young, white and middle class. They were waiting for the main act when a black man ambled across the stage with a guitar and with perhaps the mention of his name, but no more, started to sing. Initially, he was met with disinterest, as support acts mostly are, but gradually the noise in the auditorium faded like static on a radio until there was only this one person, this one voice, singing with such simplicity and honesty and something more besides. A largeness only great artists possess. He sang a song no-one in the audience had heard, about Aboriginal children being taken from their parents, and followed it with an Aboriginal mother's lament for her child found dead in a prison cell. Then, with as little ceremony as he had arrived, he left. The applause began and grew, a giant thunderous wave of it. Paul Kelly, watching from the wings (at this time, he hadn't even met Archie), knew he had witnessed one of the great performances of his life. I was sitting with a young journalist who had asked me earlier in the night, 'What is journalism?' That, I said pointing to the stage—that is journalism. The chance to witness moments of significance, moments when you know a nation may be about to change course.

I got to know Archie after that. Went to the footy with him at the Aboriginal Advancement League in Northcote and watched the Koori All-stars, was present the night the final tracks were put down on his first album *Charcoal Lane*, visited him in his various homes, first at Thornbury, later in Reservoir, once even at Framlingham in his country. And we talked. Almost at once, I seemed to understand the impact of the ordeal he had undergone in emotional and possibly spiritual terms—his art was evidence of that—but there was still an important sense in which his story eluded me and defied my comprehension. However much I listened, however much I learned, it seemed I never knew more than a few bits and pieces. Like so many Aboriginal people, he had anecdotes which would be dramatic pinnacles, defining moments, for most other people that I knew; to him, they were part of everyday existence. I particularly recall him mentioning to me a story about one of his sisters. She was walking down a country road at night when a carload of hoons passed her and fired a gun in her direction—not to hit her, as I understood the story, but to scare her in the way that you might seek to scare a possum or a crow.

The truth of the matter was that Archie's story was so far beyond my experience, it was beyond my imagining. In the end, I did summon a word for it and from an unlikely place. As a kid, I had read a novel or two by Charles Dickens. At the time, stories about the squalid underbelly of Victorian England at the height of the Industrial Age didn't seem too relevant to life in country towns in Tasmania, but now images from his books returned to me with renewed force. So many of Dickens' novels are about the passage of orphans through a society that is like a high, cold wall of faces. Some of those faces when they peer down at the narrator are cruel, some are kind. That was part of Archie's story, too. One family to whom he had been handed locked him in a shed a night, like a dog. Another, the Coxes, treated him with kindness and respect. The father was Scottish. There are photos of Archie in a kilt, and long afterwards he still had an interest in Scottish music and the Gaelic language. I seem to remember him saying the old Scotsman told him to be proud of his identity.

Dickens' critics have always accused him of constructing plots that rely on fantastic coincidences. I thought so too, then Archie told me a story about his time on the streets in Sydney. An old hero told him to keep changing his name to confound the police when he was picked up for vagrancy. Meanwhile, he met a girl with whom he felt a deep empathy. They were brother and sister, and neither knew it. I once mentioned my theory about Dickens being the only writer I had read to come close to capturing the scale of the experience of the Stolen Generation to that great Yawru man Patrick Dodson, and he agreed. As a young Aboriginal

Catholic priest visiting an orphanage in West Australia, Dodson had observed a scene akin to the one where Oliver Twist holds up his empty bowl and asks for more.

Thinking further on the matter, I realised the importance of such writers. Because of Dickens, and a few people like him, we cannot think of Victorian England without summoning images of the urban poor—particularly the children. What we need in this country is an artist with similar largeness who can implant the story of the Stolen Generation, or a member thereof, in the Australian imagination. It would be a major achievement, as it is now sadly apparent that there are people in this country—among whom is the Prime Minister, John Howard—who will never imagine it for themselves.

Charles Dickens might have given me some way of under-standing Archie's story, but, even so, I have never got to the end of it, never understood its full dimensions. I had known him several years when I saw 'Secret Lives', the television documentary made about him. That's when I learned that, at the age of sixteen, he was standing on a street corner in Fitzroy when a mate pulled over in a car and invited him to get in. The car was stolen. Archie Roach was sent to prison as an accessory to the theft. I can't describe the effect of learning that had on me beyond saying that it shocked me. To the core. This man was as sensitive as any I had ever met. He had been to that dark place human beings enter when they ask the elemental question, 'Is life worth living?'; in his case, the answer had come to him not in words but as music. Bob Geldof subsequently heard him sing and said he was the voice of Australian soul. Tom Uren, the old fighter who has championed so many humanitarian causes, compared him to Paul Robeson. Generosity is the essence of Archie Roach's art, yet law I accepted —that is, law I had never challenged or sought to change—had sent him to prison. The same laws had held in place the system which had taken him, his brothers and his sisters, from their mother and father, leaving them broken and bereft. In those days,

Archie was still on the phone. I think I embarrassed us both, but I had to do something. I rang and said sorry Archie.

('Brother' was written for this book. Martin Flanagan, who is a fifth-generation Australian of Irish descent, graduated in Law from the University of Tasmania and has worked as a journalist. His next book is an historical novel inspired by the life of Tom Wills, founder of Australian Rules Football.)

13

Veronica Brady

Senior Research Fellow, University of Western Australia

IT HAS SEEMED TO me for some years that two aspects of the
Aboriginal struggle have been under-valued. One is their
continued will to survive, the other their continued efforts to
come to terms with us. There are many, perhaps too many,
theories about our troubles with the Aborigines. We can
spare a moment to consider *their* theory about *their* troubles
with us.

Bill Stanner

Stanner was a great anthropologist and a man with a compassionate heart as well as an intelligent and creative mind. It is not difficult to imagine how he would have reacted to the stories of the
stolen generations. But how do we react? Why are there so many
of us who seem unable to acknowledge the long agony of our
Aboriginal sisters and brothers, unable to apologise and listen to
what they would have us do in return for the imposition of that
agony?

Perhaps it is because we like to think of our history as a story
of 'progress' and of ourselves as decent and open-minded people
building a society in which everyone has a right to a 'fair go'.
Perhaps it is because the God (or gods) we worship is the God of
the winners who has little mercy for the losers. For we do not
really believe in forgiveness if we fail—and surely we have failed in

our relations with the first peoples of this land, peoples who, for at least 60,000 years, lived here in tune with this land (which we now seem to be destroying).

If we open our hearts and minds to their side of the story, we may begin to realise that the gods of success—of money, power and pleasure—are cruel gods. We need to learn from the people we have oppressed and despised, the Suffering Servant described by the prophet Isaiah as 'wounded for our iniquities and bruised for our sins' who points us to life rather than death. If so many of us seem to suffer from psychic numbing, perhaps it is because we are afraid to acknowledge our need to be forgiven and to forgive ourselves.

The history that really matters in this sense is not the story of the winners but the story of the losers, of all those who were defeated, oppressed, raped, humiliated and robbed of what they held sacred: their land and their community. That story matters because it reminds us of our real task as human beings; not to be rich, powerful, famous or luxurious, but to know our place in the scheme of things, to live with respect for and with others, and for and with the earth. We must be generous, compassionate and ready to learn from our mistakes.

The story of the suffering of Aboriginal and Islander peoples reminds us that we still have a long way to go. But the goal is surely to exchange the hearts of stone—the hearts of conquerers estranged from the land and its peoples and their lives—for hearts of flesh. Such hearts will know the truth that no-one is an island, that we are all part of the one continent, one common humanity. When one person suffers, we are all wounded.

(Sister Veronica Brady is a Senior Research Fellow in the Department of English at the University of Western Australia.)

Recommendations

THESE ARE THE FIFTY-FOUR recommendations made in the Report *Bringing Them Home*. It is important to read these recommendations in the context of the stories of the stolen children as they offer pathways to the solutions to the problems, and answers to the tragedies so graphically described in the stories themselves.

Recording testimonies

1. That the Council of Australian Governments ensure the adequate funding of appropriate Indigenous agencies to record, preserve and administer access to the testimonies of Indigenous people, affected by the forcible removal policies, who wish to provide their histories in audio, audio-visual or written form.

Procedure for implementation

2a. That the Council of Australian Governments establish a working party to develop a process for the implementation of the Inquiry's recommendations and to receive and respond to annual audit reports on the progress of implementation.

2b. That the Commonwealth fund the establishment of a National Inquiry audit in the Human Rights and Equal Opportunity Commission to monitor the implementation of the Inquiry's recommendations and report annually to the Council of Australian

Governments on the progress of implementation of the recommendations.

2c.   That ATSIC fund the following peak Indigenous organisations to research, prepare and provide an annual submission to the National Inquiry audit unit evaluating the progress of implementation of the Inquiry's recommendations: Secretariat of National Aboriginal and Islander Child Care (SNAICC), Stolen Generations National Secretariat, National Aboriginal Community Controlled Health Organisation (NACCHO), and National Aboriginal and Islander Legal Services Secretariat (NAILSS).

2d.   That Commonwealth, State and Territory Governments undertake to provide fully detailed and complete information to the National Inquiry audit unit annually on request concerning progress on implementation of the Inquiry's recommendations.

Components of reparations

3.   That, for the purposes of responding to the effects of forcible removals, 'compensation' be widely defined to mean 'reparation'; that reparation be made in recognition of the history of gross violations of human rights; and that the van Boven principles guide the reparation measures. Reparation should consist of:

    i) acknowledgement and apology,

    ii) guarantees against repetition,

    iii) measures of restitution,

    iv) measures of rehabilitation, and

    v) monetary compensation.

Claimants

4.   That reparation be made to all who suffered because of forcible removal policies including:

    i) individuals who were forcibly removed as children,

    ii) family members who suffered as a result of their removal,

iii) communities which, as a result of the forcible removal of children, suffered cultural and community disintegration, and

iv) descendants of those forcibly removed who, as a result, have been deprived of community ties, cultures and language, and links and entitlements to their traditional land.

Acknowledgement and apology—Parliaments and police forces

5a.   That all Australian Parliaments:

  i) officially acknowledge the responsibility of their predecessors for the laws, policies and practices of forcible removal,

  ii) negotiate with the Aboriginal and Torres Strait Islander Commission a form of words for official apologies to Indigenous individuals, families and communities and extend those apologies with wide and culturally appropriate publicity, and

  iii) make appropriate reparation as detailed in following recommendations.

5b.   That State and Territory police forces, having played a prominent role in the implementation of the laws and policies of forcible removal, acknowledge that role and, in consultation with the Aboriginal and Torres Strait Islander Commission, make such formal apologies and participate in such commemorations as are determined.

Acknowledgement and apology—Churches and others

6.   That churches and other non-government agencies which played a role in the administration of the laws and policies under which Indigenous children were forcibly removed acknowledge that role and in consultation with the Aboriginal and Torres Strait Islander Commission make such formal apologies and participate in such commemorations as may be determined.

Commemoration

7a.   That the Aboriginal and Torres Strait Islander Commission, in consultation with the Council for Aboriginal Reconciliation, arrange for a national 'Sorry Day' to be celebrated each year to commemorate the history of forcible removal and its effects.

7b.   That the Aboriginal and Torres Strait Islander Commission, in consultation with the Council for Aboriginal Reconciliation, seek proposals for further commemorating the individuals, families and communities affected by forcible removal at the local and regional levels. That proposals be implemented when a widespread consensus within the Indigenous community has been reached.

School education

8a.   That State and Territory Governments ensure that primary and secondary school curricula include substantial compulsory modules on the history and continuing effects of forcible removal.

8b.   That the Australian Institute of Aboriginal and Torres Strait Islander Studies be funded by the Commonwealth to develop these modules.

Professional training

9a.   That all professionals who work with Indigenous children, families and communities receive in-service training about the history and effects of forcible removal.

9b.   That all undergraduates and trainees in relevant professions receive, as part of their core curriculum, education about the history and effects of forcible removal.

Genocide convention

10.   That the Commonwealth legislate to implement the *Genocide Convention* with full domestic effect.

Assistance to return to country

11.   That the Council of Australian Governments ensure that appropriate Indigenous organisations are adequately funded to employ family

reunion workers to travel with clients to their country, to provide Indigenous community education on the history and effects of forcible removal and to develop community genealogies to establish membership of people affected by forcible removal.

Language, culture and history centres

12a. That the Commonwealth expand the funding of Indigenous language, culture and history centres to ensure national coverage at regional level.

12b. That where the Indigenous community so determines, the regional language, culture and history centre be funded to record and maintain local Indigenous languages and to teach those languages, especially to people, whose forcible removal deprived them of opportunities to learn and maintain their language, and to their descendants.

Indigenous identification

13. That Indigenous organisations, such as Link-Ups and Aboriginal and Islander Child Care Agencies, which assist those forcibly removed by undertaking family history research, be recognised as Indigenous communities for the purposes of certifying descent from the Indigenous people of Australia and acceptance as Indigenous by the Indigenous community.

Heads of damage

14   That monetary compensation be provided to people affected by forcible removal under the following heads:
  i) Racial discrimination,
  ii) Arbitrary deprivation of liberty,
  iii) Pain and suffering,
  iv) Abuse, including physical, sexual and emotional abuse,
  v) Disruption of family life,
  vi) Loss of cultural rights and fulfilment,

    vii) Loss of native title rights,

   viii) Labour exploitation,

     ix) Economic loss, and

      x) Loss of opportunities.

National Compensation Fund

15.   That the Council of Australian Governments establish a joint National Compensation Fund.

National Compensation Fund Board

16a.   That the Council of Australian Governments establish a Board to administer the National Compensation Fund.

16b.   That the Board be constituted by both Indigenous and non-Indigenous people appointed in consultation with Indigenous organisations in each State and Territory having particular responsibilities to people forcibly removed in childhood and their families. That the majority of members be Indigenous people and that the Board be chaired by an Indigenous person.

Procedural principles

17.   That the following procedural principles be applied in the operations of the monetary compensation mechanism:
      i) widest possible publicity,
     ii) free legal advice and representation for claimants,
    iii) no limitation period,
    iv) independent decision-making which should include the participation of Indigenous decision-makers,
     v) minimum formality,
    vi) not bound by the rules of evidence, and
   vii) cultural appropriateness (including language).

Minimum lump sum

18.   That an Indigenous person who was removed from his or her family

during childhood by compulsion, duress or undue influence be entitled to a minimum lump sum payment from the National Compensation Fund in recognition of the fact of removal. That it be a defence to a claim for the responsible government to establish that the removal was in the best interests of the child.

Proof of particular harm

19.   That upon proof on the balance of probabilities any person suffering particular harm and/or loss resulting from forcible removal be entitled to monetary compensation from the National Compensation Fund assessed by reference to the general civil standards.

Civil Claims

20.   That the proposed statutory monetary compensation mechanism not displace claimants' common law rights to seek damages through the courts. A claimant successful in one forum should not be entitled to proceed in the other.

Destruction of records prohibited

21.   That no records relating to Indigenous individuals, families or communities or to any children, Indigenous or otherwise, removed from their families for any reason, whether held by government or non-government agencies, be destroyed.

Record preservation

22a.   That all government record agencies be funded as a matter of urgency by the relevant government to preserve and index records relating to Indigenous individuals, families and/or communities and records relating to all children, Indigenous or otherwise, removed from their families for any reason.

22b.   That indexes and other finding aids be developed and managed in a way that protects the privacy of individuals and, in particular the compilation of dossiers.

Joint records taskforces

23. That the Commonwealth and each State and Territory Government establish and fund a Records Taskforce constituted by representatives from government and church and other non-government record agencies and Indigenous user services to:

> i) develop common access guidelines to Indigenous personal, family and community records as appropriate to the jurisdiction and in accordance with established privacy principles,

> ii) advise the government whether any church or other non-government record-holding agency should be assisted to preserve and index its records and administer access,

> iii) advise government on memoranda of understanding for dealing with inter-State enquiries and for the inter-State transfer of files and other information,

> iv) advise government and churches generally on policy relating to access to and uses of Indigenous personal, family and community information, and

> v) advise government on the need to introduce or amend legislation to put these policies and practices into place.

Inter-State enquiries

24. That each government, as advised by its Records Taskforce, enter into memoranda of understanding with other governments for dealing with inter-State enquiries and for the inter-State transfer of records and other information.

Minimum access standards

25. That all common access guidelines incorporate the following standards:

> i) the right of every person, upon proof of identity only, to view all information relating to himself or herself and to receive a full copy of the same,

> ii) no application fee, copying fee or other charge of any kind to be imposed,

iii) a maximum application processing period to be agreed by the Records Taskforce and any failure to comply to be amenable to review and appeal,

iv) a person denied the right of access or having any other grievance concerning his or her information to be entitled to seek a review and, if still dissatisfied, to appeal the decision or other matter free of charge,

v) the right of every person to receive advice, both orally and in writing, at the time of application about Indigenous support and assistance services available in his or her State or Territory of residence,

vi) the form of advice provided to applicants to be drafted in consultation with local Indigenous family tracing and reunion services and to contain information about the nature and form of the information to be disclosed and the possibility of distress,

vii) the right of every person to receive all personal identifying information about himself or herself including information which is necessary to establish the identity of family members (for example, parents' identifying details such as name, community of origin, date of birth),

viii) the right of every person who is the subject of a record, subject to the exception above, to determine to whom and to what extent that information is divulged to a third person.

Freedom of Information in the Northern Territory

26. That the Northern Territory Government introduce Freedom of Information legislation on the Commonwealth model.

Indigenous Family Information Service

27. That the Commonwealth and each State and Territory Government, in consultation with relevant Indigenous services and its Records Taskforce, establish an Indigenous Family Information Service to operate as a 'first stop shop' for people seeking information about the referral to records held by the government and by churches.

That these services be staffed by Indigenous people. That to support these services each government and church record agency nominate a designated contact officer.

Training

28.   That the Commonwealth and each State and Territory Government institute traineeships and scholarships for the training of Indigenous archivists, genealogists, historical researchers and counsellors.

Indigenous repositories

29a.   That, on the request of an Indigenous community, the relevant Records Taskforce sponsor negotiations between government, church and/or other non-government agencies and the relevant Indigenous language, culture and history centre for the transfer of historical and cultural information relating to that community and its members.

29b.   That the Council of Australian Governments ensure that Indigenous language, culture and history centres have the capacity to serve as repositories of personal information that the individuals concerned have chosen to place in their care and which is protected in accordance with established privacy principles.

Establishment of family tracing and reunion services

30a.   That the Council of Australian Governments ensure that Indigenous community-based family tracing and reunion services are funded in all regional centres with a significant Indigenous population and that existing Indigenous community-based services, for example health services, in smaller centres are funded to offer family tracing and reunion assistance and referral.

30b.   That the regional services be adequately funded to perform the following functions:

     i) family history research,

 ii) family tracing,

 iii) support and counselling for clients viewing their personal records,

 iv) support and counselling for clients, family members and community members in the reunion process including travel with clients,

 v) establishment and management of a referral network of professional counsellors, psychologists, psychiatrists and others as needed by clients,

 vi) advocacy on behalf of individual clients as required and on behalf of clients as a class, for example with record agencies,

 vii) outreach and publicity,

 viii) research into the history and effects of forcible removal,

 ix) Indigenous and non-Indigenous community education about the history and effects of forcible removal,

 x) engaging the service of Indigenous experts for provision of genealogical information, traditional healing and escorting and sponsoring those returning to their country of origin,

 xi) participation in training of Indigenous people as researchers, archivists, genealogists and counsellors,

 xii) participation in national networks and conferences,

 xiii) effective participation on Record Taskforces,

 xiv) support of test cases and other efforts to obtain compensation.

Return of those removed overseas

31a. That the Commonwealth create a special visa class under the *Migration Act 1951* (Commonwealth) to enable Indigenous people forcibly removed from their families and from Australia and their descendants to return to Australia and take up permanent residence.

31b. That the Commonwealth amend the *Citizenship Act 1948* (Commonwealth) to provide for the acquisition of citizenship by any person of Aboriginal or Torres Strait Islander descent.

31c. The the Commonwealth take measures to ensure the prompt implementation of the *International Transfer of Prisoners Bill 1996*.

Research

32. That the Commonwealth Government work with the national Aboriginal and Torres Strait Islander Health Council in consultation with the National Aboriginal Community Controlled Health Organisation (NACCHO) to devise a program for research and consultations to identify the range and extent of emotional and well-being effects of the forcible removal policies.

Indigenous well-being model

33a. That all services and programs provided for survivors of forcible removal emphasise local Indigenous healing and well-being perspectives.

33b. That government funding for Indigenous preventive and primary mental health (well-being) services be directed exclusively to Indigenous community-based services including Aboriginal and Islander health services, child-care agencies and substance abuse services.

33c. That all government-run mental health services work towards delivering specialist services in partnership with Indigenous community-based services and employ Indigenous mental health workers and community members respected for their healing skills.

Health professional training

34a. That government health services, in consultation with Indigenous health services and family tracing reunion services, develop in-service training for all employees in the history and effects of forcible removal.

34b. That all health and related training institutions, in consultation with Indigenous health services and family tracing and reunion services, develop undergraduate training for all students in the history and effects of forcible removal.

Mental health worker training

35. That all State and Territory Governments institute Indigenous mental health worker training through Indigenous-run programs to ensure cultural and social appropriateness.

Parenting skills

36. That the Council of Australian Governments ensure the provision of adequate funding to relevant Indigenous organisations in each region to establish parenting and family well-being programs.

Prisoner services

37. That the Council of Australian Governments ensure the provision of adequate funding to Indigenous health and medical services and family well-being programs to establish preventive mental health programs in all prisons and detention centres and to advise prison health services. That State and Territory corrections departments facilitate the delivery of these programs and advice in all prisons and detention centres.

Private collection

38a. That every church and other non-government agency which played a role in the placement and care of Indigenous children forcibly removed from their families, at the request of an Indigenous language, culture and history centre, transfer historical and cultural information it holds relating to the community or communities represented by the centre.

38b. That churches and other non-government agencies which played a role in the placement and care of Indigenous children forcibly removed from their families identify all records relating to Indigenous families and children and arrange for their preservation, indexing and access in secure storage facilities preferably, in consultation with relevant Indigenous communities and organisations, in the National Library, the Australian Institute of Aboriginal and Torres Strait Islander Studies or an appropriate State Library.

38c.   That every church and non-government record agency which played a role in the placement and care of Indigenous children forcibly removed from their families provide detailed information about its records to the relevant Indigenous Family Information Service or Services.

Application of minimum standards and common guidelines

39.   That church and other non-government record agencies implement the national minimum access standards (Recommendation 25) and apply the relevant State, Territory or Commonwealth common access guidelines (Recommendation 23).

Counselling services

40a.   That churches and other non-government welfare agencies that provide counselling and support services to those affected by forcible removal review those services, in consultation with Indigenous communities and organisations, to ensure they are culturally appropriate.

40b.   That churches and other non-government agencies which played a role in the placement and care of Indigenous children forcibly removed from their families provide all possible support to Indigenous organisations delivering counselling and support services to those affected by forcible removal.

Land holdings

41.   That churches and other non-government agencies review their land holdings to identify land acquired or granted for the purpose of accommodating Indigenous children forcibly removed from their

families and, in consultation with Indigenous people and their land councils, return that land.

Social justice

42.   That to address the social and economic disadvantages that underlie the contemporary removal of Indigenous children and young people the Council of Australian Governments,

   i) in partnership with ATSIC, the Council for Aboriginal Reconciliation, the Office of the Aboriginal and Torres Strait Islander Justice Commissioner, and Indigenous community organisations dealing with Indigenous family and children's issues, develop and implement a social justice package for Indigenous families and children, and

   ii) pursue the implementation of the recommendations of the Royal Commission into Aboriginal Deaths in Custody which address underlying issues of social disadvantage.

Self-determination

43a.   That the Council of Australian Governments negotiate with the Aboriginal and Torres Strait Islander Commission, the Aboriginal and Torres Strait Islander Social Justice Commissioner, the Secretariat of National Aboriginal and Islander Child Care, and the National Aboriginal and Islander Legal Services Secretariat national legislation establishing a framework for negotiations at community and regional levels for the implementation of self-determination in relation to the well-being of Indigenous children and young people (national framework legislation).

43b.   That the national framework legislation adopt the following principles,

   i) That the Act binds the Commonwealth and every State and Territory Government.

   ii) That within the parameters of the Act Indigenous communities are free to formulate and negotiate an agreement on measures best suited to their individual needs concerning children, young people and families.

iii) That negotiated agreements will be open to revision by negotiation.

iv) That every Indigenous community is entitled to adequate funding and other resources to enable it to support and provide for families and children and to ensure that the removal of children is the option of last resort.

v) That the human rights of Indigenous children will be ensured.

43c. That the national framework legislation authorise negotiations with Indigenous communities that so desire on any or all of the following matters,

i) the transfer of legal jurisdiction in relation to children's welfare, care and protection, adoption and/or juvenile justice to an Indigenous community, region or representative organisation,

ii) the transfer of police, judicial and/or departmental functions to an Indigenous community, region or representative organisation,

iii) the relationship between the community, region or representative organisation and the police, court system and/or administration of the State or Territory on matters relating to children, young people and families including, where desired by the Indigenous community, region or representative organisation, policy and program development and the sharing of jurisdiction, and/or

iv) the funding and other resourcing of programs and strategies developed or agreed to by the community, region or representative organisation in relation to children, young people and families.

National standards for Indigenous children

44. That the Council of Australian Governments negotiate with the Aboriginal and Torres Strait Islander Commission, the Aboriginal

and Torres Strait Islander Social Justice Commissioner, the Secretariat of National Aboriginal and Islander Child Care, and the National Aboriginal and Islander Legal Services Secretariat national legislation binding on all levels of government and on Indigenous communities, regions or representative organisations which take legal jurisdiction for Indigenous children establishing minimum standards of treatment for all Indigenous children (national standards legislation).

National standards for Indigenous children under State, Territory or shared jurisdiction

45a. That the national standards legislation include the standards recommended below for Indigenous children under State or Territory jurisdiction or shared jurisdiction.

45b. That the negotiations for national standards legislation develop a framework for the accreditation of Indigenous organisations for the purpose of performing functions prescribed by the standards.

Standard One: Best interests of the child—factors

46a. That the national standards legislation provide that the initial presumption is that the best interest of the child is to remain with his or her Indigenous family, community and culture.

46b. That the national standards legislation provide that in determining the best interests of an Indigenous child the decision maker must also consider;
   i) the need of the child to maintain contact with his or her Indigenous family, community and culture,
   ii) the significance of the child's Indigenous heritage for his or her future well-being
   iii) the views of the child and his or her family, and
   iv) the advice of the appropriate accredited Indigenous organisation.

Standard Two: When best interests are paramount

47.   That the national standards legislation provide that in any judicial or administrative decision affecting the care and protection, adoption or residence of an Indigenous child the best interest of the child is the paramount consideration.

Standard Three: When other factors apply

48.   That the national standards legislation provide that removal of Indigenous children from their families and communities by the juvenile justice system, including for the purposes of arrest, remand in custody or sentence, is to be a last resort. An Indigenous child is not to be removed from his or her family and community unless the danger to the community as a whole outweighs the desirability of retaining the held in his or her family and community.

Standard Four: Involvement of accredited Indigenous organisations

49.   That the national standards legislation provide that in any matter concerning a child the decision-maker must ascertain whether the child is an Indigenous child, and in every matter concerning an Indigenous child ensure that the appropriate accredited Indigenous organisation is consulted thoroughly and in good faith. In care and protection matters that organisation must be involved in all decision-making from the point of notification and at each stage of decision-making thereafter including whether and if so on what grounds to seek a court order. In juvenile justice matters that organisation must be involved in all decisions at every stage including bail and conditions of bail.

Standard Five: Judicial decision-making

50.   That the national standards legislation provide that in any matter concerning a child the court must ascertain whether the child is an Indigenous child, and in every case involving an Indigenous child, ensure that the child is separately represented by a representative of the child's choosing, or where the child is incapable of choosing a

representative, by the appropriate accredited Indigenous organisation.

Standard Six: Indigenous Child Placement Principle

51a. That the national standards legislation provide that, when an Indigenous child must be removed from his or her family, including for the purpose of adoption, the placement of the child, whether temporary or permanent, is to be made in accordance with the Indigenous Child Placement Principle.

51b. Placement is to be made according to the following order of preference:

   i) placement with a member of the child's family (as defined by local custom and practice) in the correct relationship to the child in accordance with Aboriginal or Torres Strait Islander law,

   ii) placement with a member of the child's community in a relationship of responsibility for the child according to local custom and practice,

   iii) placement with another member of the child's community, or

   iv) placement with another Indigenous carer.

51c. The preferred placement may be displaced where:

   i) that placement would be detrimental to the child's best interests,

   ii) the child objects to that placement, or

   iii) no carer in the preferred category is available.

51d. Where placement is with a non-Indigenous carer the following principles must determine the choice of carer:

   i) family reunion is a primary objective,

   ii) continuing contact with the child's Indigenous family, community and culture must be ensured, and

   iii) the carer must live in proximity to the child's Indigenous family and community.

51e.   No placement of an Indigenous child is to be made except on the advice and with the recommendation of the appropriate accredited Indigenous organisation. Where the parents of the child disagree with the recommendation of the appropriate accredited Indigenous organisation, the court must determine the best interests of the child.

Standard Seven: Adoption a last resort

52.   That the national standards legislation provide that an order for adoption of an Indigenous child is not to be made unless adoption is in the best interests of the child and that adoption of an Indigenous child be an open adoption unless the court or other decision-maker is satisfied that an open adoption would not be in the best interests of the child. The terms of an open adoption order should remain reviewable at any time at the insistence of any party.

Standard Eight: Juvenile justice

53a.   That the national standards legislation incorporate the following rules to be followed in every matter involving an Indigenous child or young person.

53b.   That the national standards legislation provide that evidence obtained in breach of any of the following rules is to be inadmissible against the child or young person except at the insistence of the child or young person himself or herself.

Rule 1: Warnings

Arrest and charge are actions of last resort. Subject to Rule 2, a police officer is to issue a warning, without charge, to a child or young person reasonably suspected of having committed an offence without requiring the child or young person to admit the offence and without imposing any penalty or obligation on the child or young person as a condition of issuing the warning.

Rule 2: Summons, attendance notice

A child or young person may be charged with an offence when the alleged offence is an indictable offence. The charging officer must secure the suspect's attendance at the court hearing in relation to the charge by issuing a summons or attendance notice unless the officer has a reasonable belief that the suspect is about commit a further indictable offence or, due to the suspect's previous conduct, that the suspect may not comply with a summons or attendance notice.

Rule 3: Notification

When a child or young person has been arrested or detained the responsible officer must notify the appropriate accredited Indigenous organisation immediately of the fact of the arrest and make arrangements for the attendance of a representative of that organisation.

Rule 4: Consultation

The responsible officer, in accordance with Standard 4, must consult thoroughly and in good faith with the appropriate accredited Indigenous organisation as to the appropriate means of dealing with every child or young person who has been arrested or detained.

Rule 5: Interrogation

No suspect of witness is to be interviewed in relation to an alleged offence unless:

i) a parent or person responsible for the suspect or witness is present, unless the suspect of witness refuses to be interviewed in the presence of such a person or such a person is not reasonably available,

ii) a legal adviser chosen by the suspect or witness or, where he or she is not capable of choosing a legal adviser, a representative of the appropriate accredited Indigenous organisation is present, and

iii) an interpreter is present in every case in which the suspect or witness does not speak English as a first language.

Rule 6: Caution

No suspect or witness is to be interviewed in relation to an alleged offence unless:

> i) the caution has been explained in private to the suspect or witness by his or her legal adviser or representative,
>
> ii) the interviewing officer has satisfied himself or herself that the suspect or witness understands the caution, and
>
> iii) the suspect or witness freely consents to be interviewed.

Rule 7: Withdrawal of consent

The interview is to be immediately discontinued when the suspect or witness has withdrawn his or her consent.

Rule 8: Recording

The interview must be recorded on audio tape or audiovisual tape. The tape must include the pre-interview discussions between the suspect of witness and the interviewing officer in which the officer must satisfy himself or herself that the suspect or witness understands the caution and freely consents to be interviewed.

Rule 9: Bail

Unconditional bail is a right. The right to bail without condition can only be valid where conditions are reasonably believed due to the suspect's past conduct to be necessary to ensure the suspect will attend court as notified. The right to bail can only be withdrawn where it is reasonably believed, due to the nature of the alleged offence or because of threats having been made by the suspect, that remand in custody is necessary in the interests of the community as a whole.

Rule 10: Bail review

The suspect has a right to have the imposition of bail conditions or the refusal of bail reviewed by a senior police officer. In every case in which the senior officer refuses to release the suspect on bail, the officer must immediately notify a magistrate, bail justice or other authorised independent person who is to conduct a bail hearing forthwith. The suspect is to be represented at that hearing by a legal adviser of his or her choice or, where incapable of choosing, by a representative of the appropriate accredited Indigenous organisation.

Rule 11: Bail hostels

When bail has been refused the suspect is to be remanded in the custody of an Indigenous bail hostel, group home or private home administered by the appropriate accredited Indigenous organisation unless this option is not available in the locality.

Rule 12: Detention in police cells

No suspect is to be confined in police cells except in extraordinary and unforeseen circumstances which prevent the utilisation of alternatives. Every suspect confined in police cells overnight is to be accompanied by an Indigenous person in a relationship of responsibility to the suspect.

Rule 13: Non-custodial sentences

Custodial sentences are an option of last resort. Every child or young person convicted of an offence who, in accordance with Rule 14 cannot be dismissed without sentence, is to be sentenced to a non-custodial program administered by the appropriate accredited Indigenous organisation or by an Indigenous community willing to accept the child. The child's consent to be dealt with in this way is required. The selection of the appropriate program is to be made on the advice of the appropriate accredited Indigenous organisation and, where possible, the child's family.

Rule 14: Sentencing factors

The sentencer must take into account:
  i) the best interests of the child or young person,
  ii) the wishes of the child or young person's family and community,
  iii) the advice of the appropriate accredited Indigenous organisation,

iv) the principle that Indigenous children are not to be removed from their families and communities except in extraordinary circumstances, and

v) Standard 3.

Rule 15: Custodial sentences

Where the sentencer, having taken into account all of the factors stipulated in Rule 14, determines that a custodial sentence is necessary, the sentence must be for the shortest appropriate period of time and the sentencer must provide its reasons in writing to the State or Territory Attorney General and the appropriate accredited Indigenous organisation. No child or young person is to be given an indeterminate custodial sentence or mandatory sentence.

Family law

54. That the Family Law Act 1975 (Commonwealth) be amended by,

i) including in section 60B(2) a new paragraph (ba) 'children of Indigenous origins have a right, in community with other members of their group, to enjoy their own culture, profess and practise their own religion, and use their own language', and

ii) replacing in section 68F(2)(f) the phrase 'any need' with the phrase 'the need of every Aboriginal and Torres Strait Islander child'.

Afterword

THE RAPING AND ABDUCTION of women and the stealing of children have always been part of the story of conquest—acts that brutally illustrate new, imposed relationships of dominance, submission and humiliation.

In Australia the European colonists took Aboriginal children away from their kinsfolk, from the earliest days of colonisation. The practice was denounced officially by governors and unofficially by settlers concerned about the ethics of colonisation. In 1819 William Sorell, the Lieutenant Governor of Van Diemen's Land (Tasmania) issued a proclamation condemning the behaviour of the settlers and the cruelties practised which, he described as 'repugnant to Humanity and disgraceful to the British character'. He was particularly concerned that the 'miscreants' in remote districts pursued the women ' for the purpose of compelling them to abandon their children'. This outrage, Sorell declared, was the most certain to 'excite in the sufferers a strong thirst for revenge against all white men'.

But the concern of humanitarians had little effect on the ways things happened out on the frontier where the stealing of women and children was a constant corollary of the punitive expedition. The Queensland Native Police officers were well known as suppliers of Indigenous children. When taxed about this government officials explained that they could do little to stop the trade in children because it was so profitable, that there was a ready market and that many settlers were eager to buy a young boy or girl. It was customary for stockmen, drovers and teamsters to travel with young boys or girls. The wisdom of the frontier was that girls were as useful as boys around the camp, were less likely to run away, and provided sexual services to the womenless white men.

The consequences of abduction and illicit adoption were clearly apparent from the earliest years of settlement. Young children appeared to adapt quickly to their new surroundings. But in early adolescence they rebelled as they understood their circumstances and the fact that they were treated as unpaid servants rather than as family members. They became 'unmanageable' and usually ran away either to return to their own people or to live on the fringe of settler society, alienated from both the colonists and the Indigenes.

For all their talk about 'civilising' and 'saving' and 'uplifting' the Indigenous people, white Australia could not accept Aborigines as equals even when they had grown up in European society and had received a western education. The caste barrier was impenetrable. Those who had most reason to assume they could become part of settler society were more rather than less likely to become objects of derision and abuse.

It was tragic that when, in the twentieth century, state and federal governments decided to remove children from their families they repeated most of the mistakes and cruelties perpetrated by individuals in the colonial period. And government was able to take action on a much larger scale. Having wrenched the children away from their kin and culture, government departments had so little to offer. They never spent sufficient money on their Indigenous wards. Anything was good enough for them. Food and clothing were inadequate. Staff were usually unqualified. Zealots and misfits often ended up as supervisors and teachers. Education was inferior, and often deliberately so. Governments flagrantly disregarded their duty of care.

It was taken for granted that Aborigines could aspire only to unskilled labour of the most demeaning kind, that an educated Aborigine was an anomaly who could never find an appropriate place in white society. What was more, educated Aborigines were potential troublemakers and agitators. In frontier folk lore no one was more hated than the 'half-educated mission boy'. So-called cheeky or uppity 'niggers' were treated with ruthless brutality in order to keep them 'in their place'.

It is true that government officials and politicians were often 'well-meaning'. They had concern and compassion for individuals. But Aborigines have suffered almost as much over the past two hundred years from misguided benevolence as from the actions of those with evil intent. Pervasive racism when combined with coercive authority was an enormously destructive force. When it became involved in the desire to preserve a white Australia and to 'breed out the colour' the consequences were tragic for thousands of Aboriginal families all over the country.

The testimony and the pain that are reproduced in this book will allow all Australians to learn about one of the most distressing chapters in the troubled history of settler Australia's relations with the 'first nations' of this land. It is also a story of determination and survival, courage and forgiveness that Indigenous Australia offers up as a gesture of reconciliation.

Henry Reynolds
Hobart
December 1997

Postscript

THE PRESENT FEDERAL GOVERNMENT persists in its refusal to apologise to the people of the stolen generations for the practices and policies of past governments with regard to Indigenous people. It is possible to register an apology on <http://apology.west.net.au/>

The following poem was written by Millicent whose story is recorded in this book.

SORRY

Years have come and years have gone
And we still don't know where we belong.
Our future was placed in strangers' hands
Who took us away, away from the land.
Decisions were made where we would live
Deprived of security a family could give.
A neglected future and a lost past.
It's a wonder any of us did last
To tell our stories of a stolen generation.
All this was done without justification.

Chorus
We know it was one of white man's tragic mistakes.
Why can't they say SORRY for goodness sakes?
one little five-letter word.
We are all waiting
But it won't be heard.
For all of the children of the stolen generation

Let the word SORRY be heard across our nation.
They want us to forgive and forget
But they still haven't said SORRY yet.
To say SORRY to the aboriginal people across our nation
Would be a giant step into reconciliation.

Some of us have found families at last
But it hasn't erased nightmares from the past.
For some of us are accepted and re-unite.
For some of is it is still an on-going fight.
Too many years have passed us by.
But we are not giving up without a try
To be a family and have memories to share
If it takes forever we don't care.
We have waited so long to be together
We are strong enough to face any stormy weather.
We were stolen away
We had no choice
Now let's find our families and all rejoice!

Millicent